JAPAN INC.

JAPAN INC.

An Introduction to
Japanese Economics
Volume 2
(The Comic Book)

Shotaro Ishinomori

Translated by Alan G. Gleason

Lanchester Press Inc.
Sunnyvale CA
http://www.lanchester.com

The persons and organizations appearing in this book are entirely fictitious and have no relation to actual persons or organizations.

Lanchester Press Inc.

Published in Japan by Nihon Keizai Shimbun, Inc.
Reprinted with permission of Nihon Keizai Shimbun, Inc.

ISBN 1-57321-006-4

Library of Congress Card Number: 96-78393

Translator: Alan G. Gleason
Electronic imaging: Costas Schuler
Printed and bound by Patson's Press Inc., Sunnyvale, California.
Lanchester Press Inc., P.O. Box 60621, Sunnyvale, California 94086 USA.

CONTENTS

Preface to the American Edition

Volume Two of the epic business manga series *Japan Inc. (Manga Nihon Keizai Nyumon)* was published in 1987, at the height of the Japanese "economic bubble" of the Eighties. The bubble had burst by 1991, but not before Japan and the United States had passed through an unprecedented decade of frenzied economic competition and grudging co-dependence.

In this volume, writer Shotaro Ishinomori has cleverly woven together four of the more dramatic subplots in this relationship. Here we are treated to a Japanese insider's view of efforts by American banks to the break into Japan's financial market; the response of Japanese automakers to the anti-import backlash in the U.S.; opening skirmishes in the war between American and Japanese computer makers; and the flirtation with unorthodox business cycle theories and strategies by investors on both sides of the Pacific.

Together these scenarios provide the reader with a fascinating cross-section of the frenetic decade that was the Roaring Eighties. Of course even in the wake of twin recessions in Japan and the U.S., these scenarios continue to unfold in unpredictable ways, as we'll see in Volumes 3 and 4 of Ishinomori's saga.

CAST OF CHARACTERS

Hiroshi Okada (age 30)
A graduate of the elite Tokyo University, Okada works in the Planning Office of Goyo Bank, one of Japan's largest city banks, where he has the key assignment of drafting plans for the bank's future growth. The bank sent Okada to Harvard Business School, where he met Sawako Matsumoto.

Tatsuo Homma (age 45)
Chief of the Investigative Section of the Minister's Secretariat at the Ministry of Finance, Homma is a bureaucrat with a conscience who enjoys the confidence of his mentor, Professor Soichiro Funaoka. Homma agonizes over the conflict between the obligations of the government to its citizens and the fiscal constraints under which it must operate. He and Sawako Matsumoto were classmates in Funaoka's seminar.

Sawako Matsumoto (age 29)
Born in Wakayama Prefecture near Osaka and a graduate of the prestigious Kyoto University, Sawako attended Harvard Business School, then remained in the U.S. to work at Manhattan Trust, one of America's leading banks. After handling the bank's European and Latin American accounts, she has been reassigned to Manhattan Trust's Japan branch.

Soichiro Funaoka (age 62)
Funaoka is a professor at the Economic Research Institute of Kyoto University, where he was Sawako Matsumoto's mentor. A leading authority on Japanese economics, he once served on numerous advisory councils, but withdrew from public life out of disgust with bureaucratic turf wars and political corruption. He now spends his days absorbed in research at his home in the Higashiyama district of Kyoto.

Hashimoto (Director of the Banking Bureau, Ministry of Finance)

James Miller (Chairman of Manhattan Trust)

zaki
ief of the Planning
ice, Goyo Bank)

Morikawa (employee at the U.S plant of Toyote Motors)

Bob (employee at th
Japan office of Manhattan Trust)

Furuichi (President of Goyo Bank)

Suzuki (salesman at Matsudai Motors)

① Banking Fiasco

"False face must hide what the false heart doeth know."—
Shakespeare, *Macbeth.*

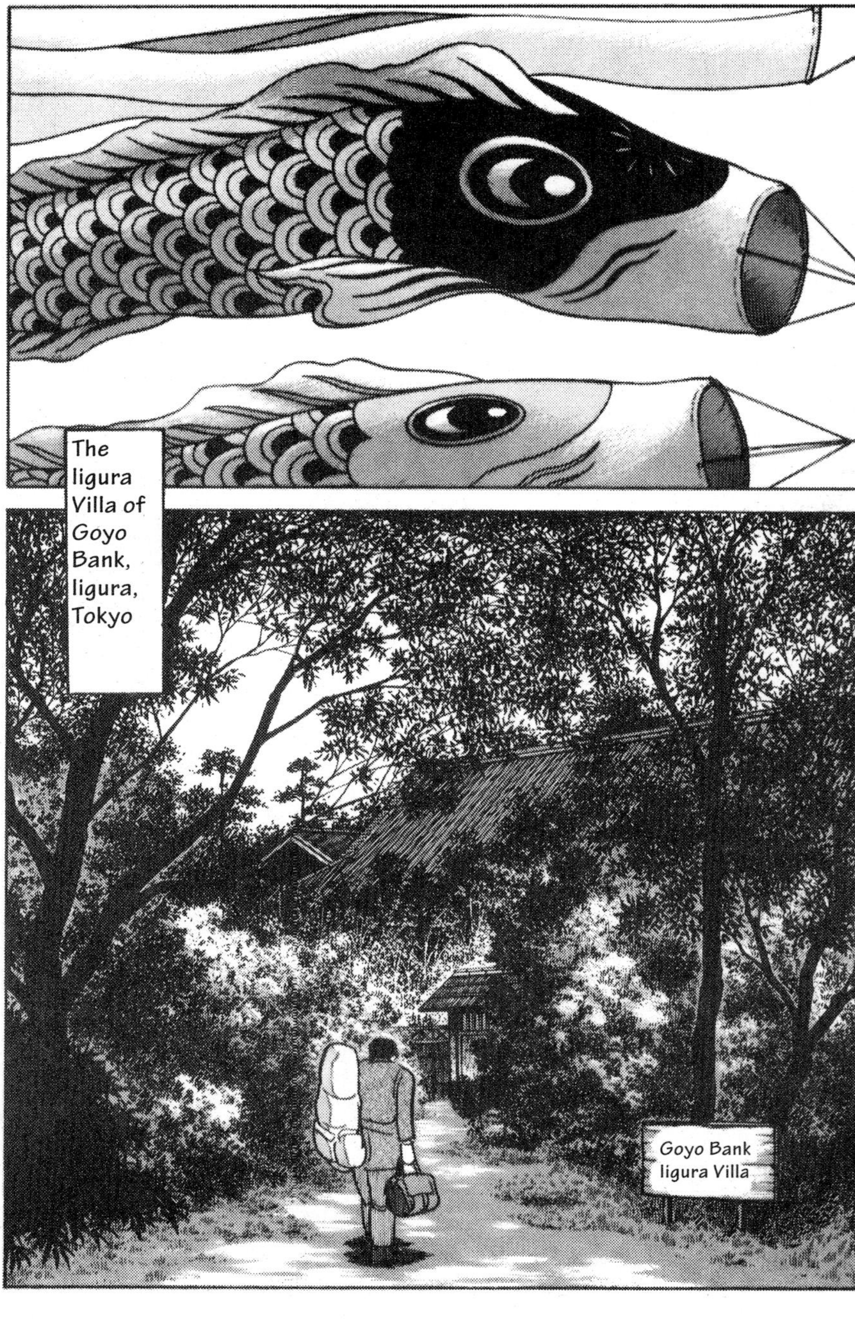
The Iigura Villa of Goyo Bank, Iigura, Tokyo
Goyo Bank Iigura Villa

'Morning.
'Morning.
If he's calling a meeting on a Sunday
I guess things must be reaching the boiling point, eh!
And on top of that
he orders us to pretend we're going out to play golf...
Well, that's typical of the Chief.
Yeah, if the media gets wind of it, the whole thing could blow up in our faces !
The Chief also told us to come prepared
to spend the night here...
KREE!

CENTRAL BANK: The central institution of the financial system of a country, usually established by special legislation. The Bank of England, the Deutsche Bundesbank of Germany, the Federal Reserve System of the United States, and the Bank of Japan are all central banks.

You've probably all guessed why I asked you to come here today...
We're approaching the final stage of negotiations over Taigen Mutual Savings Bank.
So things are coming to a head already, are they?!
That's correct. First, I'd like our MOF man, Okada, to give us an update on the situation...
Yes sir.

Last night, the president and managing director of Taigen were summoned to the Finance Ministry.
My contact there says the MOF served them with a final notice at the meeting.
Hmm. We know Taigen's been undergoing a full-scale inspection since last month...
Right. Apparently, the purpose of the meeting was to discuss the results of the inspection.
That bad, huh?!
What did the MOF tell them?
The MOF's keeping mum about it, but it's clearly worse than expected if they're calling the president up on the carpet like that...
FLICK
That they have no choice but to merge with another bank!
Apparently, the Banking Bureau chief told the president in no uncertain terms—If you don't agree to this, the MOF won't lift a finger
to bail you out!
Just as we predicted.

MOF: Ministry of Finance. "MOF man" Hiroshi Okada is in charge of spying on the MOF. The Finance Ministry and the Bank of Japan are supposed to be jointly responsible for overseeing Japan's banks, but the BOJ's influence is said to be on the wane in recent years.

But have they made
the resignation of the bank's entire management a precondition?
Oh yes, that's understood. The top brass at Taigen were hand-picked by the owners.
They had a direct hand in the owners' reckless lending practices, so they have to go too.
So how does the MOF view us
as a prospective match for Taigen?!
I'm absolutely sure the Banking Bureau chief sees us as the best possible candidate for a merger.
It'll look good for him if he can take care of one more problem bank amid all this talk about streamlining the industry.
The only banks strong enough to absorb Taigen are us, Chiyoda, and Asahi Bank, right?

So they're not giving any thought to combining two mutual savings banks, say,
instead of merging Taigen with a city bank like ours?
Not for the time being, I believe.
Maybe if the merger was of two sound, top-ranking banks— but with Taigen we're talking about a bank saddled with a huge load of bad loans !
If word gets out and the depositors start panicking, it'll be too late to do anything...
No wonder MOF wants to move fast.
Any movement by Chiyoda or Asahi?
Nothing we can see at the moment...
If you look at Taigen's branches and their loan customers,
there would be a lot of overlap for Chiyoda or Asahi, so it's not such a good deal for them.

CITY BANK: A nationwide bank based in one of Japan's major cities. There are thirteen city banks: Dai-Ichi Kangyo, Fuji, Sumitomo, Mitsubishi, Sanwa, Mitsui, Tokai, Taiyo Kobe, Yamato, Kyowa, Saitama, Hokkaido Takushoku, and Tokyo.

Taigen is based in Tokyo,
and it has its strongest presence in the old city neighborhoods.
That's why the MOF regards us as the prime candidate.
Besides, we can hardly stand idly by while some other city bank snatches Taigen up!
For an Osaka-based bank like ours,
it's a good fit to the areas where we're deficient.
The question is...
Can we pay for it, or not?!
Exactly!
That's why I've gathered you all here today.
I want you to come up with an estimate of Taigen's nonperforming loans. Also, think about how we'd deal with redundant branches and the personnel problems involved with merging staffs.

I also think it's crucial to anticipate the reaction from Taigen's loan customers.
We don't want them to join forces with the labor unions and try to squelch the merger.
Yeah, that's what happened to Sumiyoshi Bank just when it was all set to merge!
Right, right!
Now listen, everyone!
There's going to be an emergency managing directors' meeting tomorrow afternoon. I want you to have some hard data on these points ready by then!
Give it your best shot, even if it means staying up all night tonight.
Will do, Chief!

MONETARY POLICY: Planned adjustments in the money supply for the purpose of stabilizing prices, rectifying trade imbalances, and so on. In Japan, this function is performed by the Finance Ministry and the Bank of Japan.

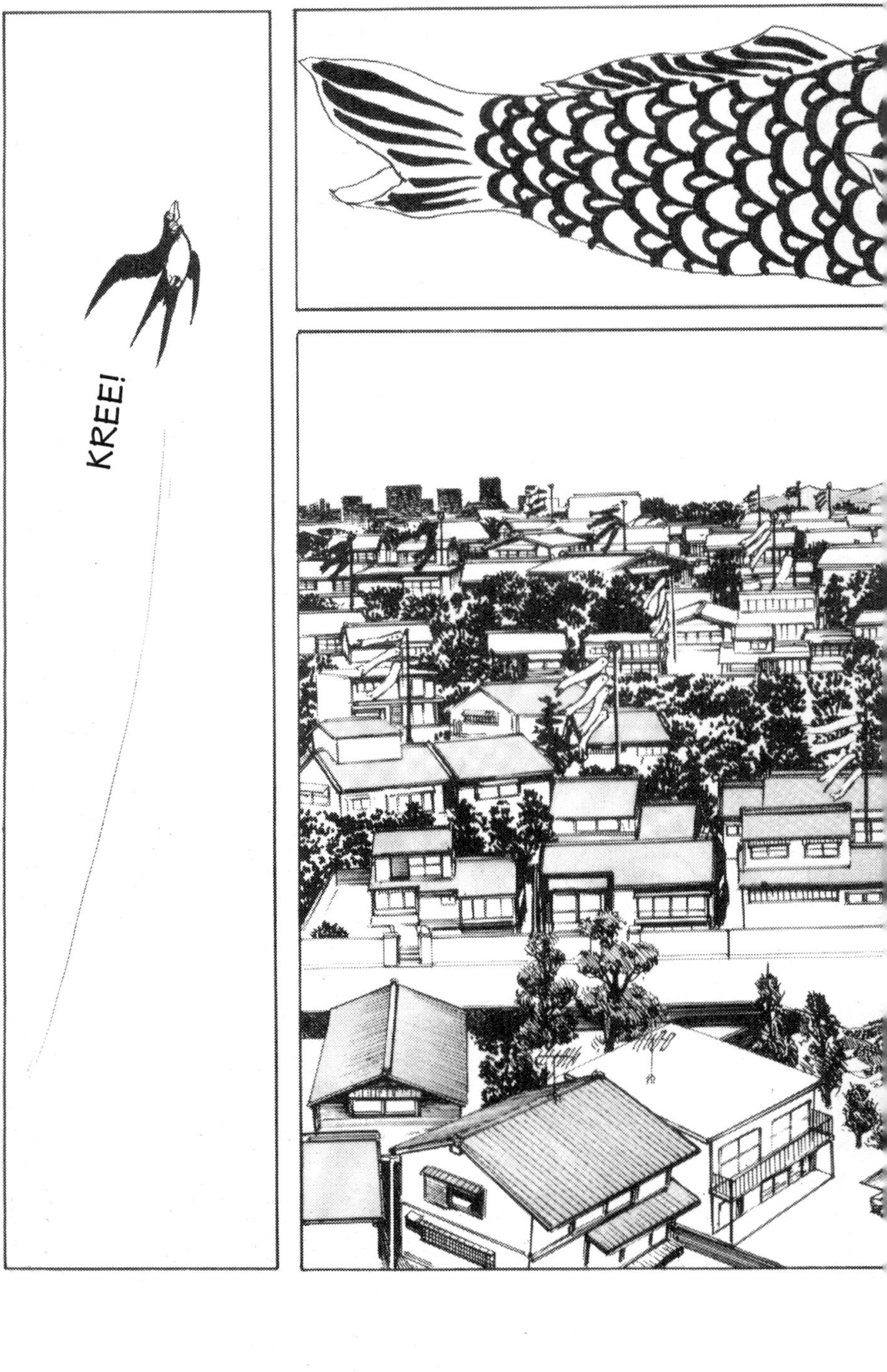
KREE!

IIGURA
VILLA
Whew...
Are you sure this figure's right—we'd have to write off 70 billion yen in bad loans ?!

MONETARY INSTRUMENT: Means of regulating the money supply, including discount rate, reserve requirement, and open market operations. As Japan undergoes further financial deregulation and internationalization, and corporate financial structures grow stronger, traditional monetary policies are less effective.

That's the figure the MOF gave us.
But we won't know the real story unless we check things out for ourselves.
Trouble is, by the time we've seen the real picture, warts and all...
it'll be too late to back out of the merger.
Well, that would be a decision for the top brass to make.
One thing, though...
Bureaucrats tend to apply different standards of judgement than what we use in the real world.
I think there's a big difference between initiating a merger ourselves, and agreeing to a merger at the request of the MOF.
Hm?
In other words, what can we get out of the MOF as a condition for acquiring Taigen —
Right?
The key people at the Ministry
have worked out a blueprint for restructuring this country's banking system.

The current structure can't last much longer—
not just for the regional and mutual banks, but the city banks too!
The MOF intends to reduce the number of city banks to fewer than ten...
at least, that's what I'm told.
If that happens, competition with Chiyoda, Asahi, and the other top banks
is going to get really vicious!
I expect calls to "observe customary practices"
SPLASH
will fall on deaf ears when that happens, eh.
No doubt. We'll have to conserve our resources just to make it through the coming war. That's something we can't lose sight of with respect to the Taigen question, either.
You're absolutely right.
By the way, Okada...
I heard some disturbing news from a financial journalist acquaintance of mine the other day.
Yes?
He says there's an American bank that has its eyes
on Taigen!!

DISCOUNT RATE OPERATIONS: The official discount rate is the interest rate charged by the Bank of Japan when lending funds to commercial banks. The BOJ influences the lending rates charged by these banks by raising or lowering its discount rate, thus indirectly speeding up or slowing down business investment activity.

WHAT?!
Are you sure?!
Who is it?!
One of the biggest banks in the U.S. — Manhattan Trust!
M-Manhattan Trust ?!
Yeah, if it's Manhattan, I can believe it.
It doesn't surprise me they'd be attracted to Japan, with our high savings rate!
Manhattan's current chairman, James Miller, has gotten great results in a short time by focusing on consumer finance.
......
They're known in the States for their strength in product development— expanding their customer base
by coming out with one new personal banking service after another...
Of all the foreign banks making inroads into Japan, Manhattan's got the most impressive staff!
They have several officers who are fluent in Japanese... One even has a reputation for belting out Japanese firemen's chants!

You mean, like in those volunteer firemen's parades?!
Yep, that's how much they're into doing business here...
which is why this story I heard sounds credible.
So by acquiring Taigen they gain a foothold here, picking up an entire branch network at one shot...
You're right, it's a perfectly plausible scenario!
According to this reporter,
they're dispatching a Japanese staffer over
here to take charge of their buyout strategy.
Come to think of it, so do you, right?
Why? Does that ring a bell for you?
I think he said she has an M.B.A. from Harvard.
A woman, as a matter of fact...
What?!
A Japanese female working for Manhattan ...?!
That's right.

There was one girl in my class
who went to work for Manhattan.
If this employee is a Japanese woman—
She must be the one !
Her name was Sawako Matsumoto...
FLICK
Apparently she's quite young.
If it's Sawako,
she's not even thirty.
Even for an American bank, that takes a lot of nerve —
Hmph!
sending over such a young woman! Well, it's just a rumor...
PUFF PUFF
Sawako Matsumoto dispatched to Japan...!
Chief!
She could definitely be the one, from what I know of her!
Hm?
......

Why? Is she that talented?
Heh heh heh.
What happened, Okada?
You get trounced by her in one of those famous Harvard debates?
Urk!
Uh, no...
Okay, lemme guess. She jilted you, is that it?
>GULP<
...No, nothing like that !!
Ha ha ha!
Gotcha!
I see... well, at any rate you're acquainted with her, eh!
That's a good break for us...
Use it to your advantage, and keep a close eye on her!
We can't afford to ignore these rumors about Manhattan!
Yessir!
Now then, we better get some shuteye.
It's almost sunrise.
......

It's been six years already...!
After I got the top score on that study-abroad exam at Goyo Bank...

they sent me to Harvard Business School.
I was thrilled and scared, all at once.
It was my first time abroad...
The curriculum was so tough,
even the Americans in my class were ready to throw in the towel...

RESERVE REQUIREMENT OPERATIONS: The reserve requirement is the percentage of bank deposits that the Bank of Japan requires commercial banks to keep in no-interest deposits at the BOJ. The BOJ adjusts the amount of money in the financial market by raising or lowering its reserve requirement.

Every day was the same. All I did was study and sleep...
But then I met Sawako Matsumoto!
She had such a beautiful smile ... I fell for her on the spot!
But I was no match for her, either in English ability or scholastic achievement.

That was a shock for me. No one had ever out-studied me before.
But Sawako was always one step ahead of me!
That sense of rivalry finally got in the way of my attraction to her..
And now Sawako's coming home —
as my rival in business, no less!
Well, this time, I can't let her beat me !!

Goyo Bank headquarters, Otemachi, Tokyo
GOYO BANK

The Planning Office, where Hiroshi Okada works, is on the 19th floor.
The Planning Office of a Japanese bank is not concerned with the bank's primary business of managing deposits and loans. Instead, it is a highly political entity that handles strategy vis-a-vis the Finance Ministry and coordinates joint actions and public relations efforts with other banks. In short, the Planning Office is responsible for manipulating information. If the president of a bank becomes chairman of the Federation of Bankers Associations, for example, his Planning Office must shoulder the task of balancing the interests of all the member banks.
Okada is the youngest member of the Planning Office at Goyo, but widely regarded as the most talented.
Listen up, everyone!
At the managing directors' meeting yesterday, they formally decided to get moving on the acquisition of Taigen Mutual.
Hoo boy!
That means the first thing we have to do
is set up a meeting between our President and the head of the Banking Bureau.
Gulp!

Right. Okada, I want you to approach them about the possibility of a discreet meeting sometime this week.
Also, we've got to familiarize the President with the terms we'll be offering them, so I'll need a memo on that right away.
Yessir!
TAP TAP
They must 've decided that Taigen's branch network was too good to pass up!
Yep, it would be a helluva lot harder to come up with the funds
to open up that many branches from scratch!
It's the trend of the times. We've got to shift our focus from wholesale banking for businesses —
to retail banking for individual customers.
This merger should be a big step in that direction...
Taigen Mutual has a presence in the service and retail shopping sectors...
They can keep their branches open till 7 p.m., so they do a lot of evening business with city-dwellers...
Of course, we don't know if we can get permission
to keep our branches open till 7 after the merger...

Well, that'll be a major negotiating point, I expect.
If we get our way, we can use it as a wedge to keep more and more branches open till 7!
And we'd be the only city bank who could make that claim!
You think they'll give us that, though?
We may be entering the age
of the banking convenience store!
Well,
when they relaxed banking regulations in Europe, late-night banks sprang up all over the place!
You can bet our competitors are thinking along the same lines...
Maybe we should find out what they're up to.
Never mind, I'll check into that myself!
I've got other things to check...

WHOLESALE/RETAIL BANKING: Wholesale banking refers to large-scale lending to corporations for capital investment purposes, while retail banking refers to small loans to individuals for housing and the like.

Narita
Airport

Welcome to Japan!
Sawako!!
Why, Bob!
HA HA HA
Welcome home!
Or I guess I should say ...

WINDOW GUIDANCE: The Bank of Japan's practice of orally advising commercial banks every quarter on the amount each bank should lend over the next three months. "Window guidance" is an effective means by which the BOJ controls the banks. [This practice was discontinued in 1991 — Ed.]

It's sweet of you to come all the way out here!
Hey, how could I not, when my favorite gal's coming back home?!
I might forget to meet Chairman Miller, but I'd never forget to meet you!
I gotta tell ya, Sawako—
STARE
Hm?
You look prettier every time I see you!
It was worth the wait—glad I didn't get hitched!
Yeah, right, Bob!
This must be the fourth or fifth time you "didn't get hitched," right?!
You old playboy, you!
How many poor Japanese girls' hearts have you broken since you came here, anyway —
Ha ha ha! Sharp-tongued as ever, aren'tcha, Sawako!
By the way, I made a reservation for you at a hotel in Tokyo...
Thank you! I hardly feel like I'm coming "home," you know... Tokyo's like a foreign place to me after all these years!

I'm going to have to depend on you to show me around, Bob!
HA HA
Japanese Sawako asks Gaijin Bob
to help get her oriented — that's a twist! But I guess that's what Tokyo's all about these days...
Just wait there a minute, okay?
I'll bring the car around.
Sawako Matsumoto, isn't it?
Remember me? Hiroshi Okada— we were at school together in Boston!
Hiroshi! Of course!!

OPEN MARKET OPERATION: The buying and selling of securities, bills, etc. on the financial market by the Bank of Japan. Selling bonds removes money from the market, while buying them injects money into it.

It's been ages!
What great luck!
I never guessed I'd run into an old friend as soon as I stepped off the plane...
Yeah, I'm here to pick up a friend coming in from the States ...
Who'd have thought we'd bump into each other here, of all places?
So, Sawako —
I hear you went to work for ... Manhattan Trust, was it?
That's right, but
I've been transferred to Japan now.
No kidding! What sort of work will you be doing?
Who knows, maybe we'll be competitors!
Oh no, I don't even know yet exactly what I'll be doing...
I hope to take my time figuring out what needs to be done.
I have absolutely no experience doing business in Japan.
So I'll be starting from scratch.
Oh, come on!
If they're transferring you back to Japan

CREDIT CEILING SYSTEM: The Bank of Japan imposes a fixed lending limit on financial institutions to prevent their excessive dependence on the BOJ for loans. The BOJ currently applies this ceiling to ten city banks which are particularly prone to borrowing from the central bank.

after your great work for them in a cutthroat market like New York,
they must have some big plans for you and Manhattan Trust over here ... am I right?!
But I don't have anywhere near that sort of ability...
Ha ha ha! You flatter me, Hiroshi!
Well, I'd be glad to ! After all, I owe it to you.
You're the one who always helped me out in business school!
In fact, I hope you'll share some of your expertise with me!
....
Oh, please, you don't owe me a thing!
I feel like I'm being audacious
Your assertive attitude was a great inspiration to me!
to even think of doing business in Tokyo with people as talented as you are!
Audacious, eh...

So just what sort of "audacious" undertakings do you have planned?! Maybe something like —
taking over a Japanese bank?!
What?!
Oops, looks like your ride's here.
BEEP BEEP
Well,
I have to go meet my plane now anyway ...
But let's plan on having dinner together sometime, okay?
Uh, sure, that would be nice ...
Talk to you soon!
Goodbye...
......

Who was that ?
A classmate of mine from business school...
SLAM
He's one of the elite at Goyo bank.
It's third among city banks in total deposits, and tops in profits.
......
Goyo?
Huh!
No wonder he acted like such a snob!
Why? Is Goyo doing all that well?
Goyo's viewed as the vanguard of the financial revolution in this country. Mark my words! They'll overtake Chiyoda, which seems happy to coast on its old zaibatsu connections,
They're known for ruthless efficiency and innovative management...
and Asahi, which is still recovering from its merger with another city bank
—and become the all-around Number One! It's just a matter of time!
I see.
I guess going up against someone like that is asking for trouble, then...

EXCLUSIVE FUNCTIONS OF BANKS: Refers to the three principal functions of banks: deposits, loans, and exchange transactions. Recently, as securities companies move into areas traditionally the domain of banks, the term "exclusive" has become somewhat moot.

Sawako, is your work here so important you can't even tell *me* about it?!
No, no, I don't have anything like that in mind!
Wha - ?! Are you planning to...
Well, I don't even know how important it is myself yet...
Once I get a better idea, I'll be asking you for advice, believe me.
So I can't help figuring it's a pretty big deal!
chose you specifically for this job...
I hear Chairman Miller
......

FUJIYA
SONY
An exclusive restaurant in Tokyo

AUXILIARY FUNCTIONS OF BANKS: Other tasks that invariably accompany the "exclusive" functions of banks. Japan's New Banking Law mentions several such functions, including guarantees of obligations, buying and selling securities, underwriting new security issues, and acquisition of money claims.

Banking Bureau Director Hashimoto of the Ministry of Finance
President Furuichi of Goyo Bank
SPLASH
You think they're going to make a final decision today?
Let's hope so.
But don't forget— the Ota family, which owns Taigen, has its claws sunk deep in the ruling party.
I've heard they've got some powerful friends exerting pressure on their behalf ove a number of issues

Settling loans to their cronies' businesses, separating their personal assets from the bank's...
They could prove to be a bit of a problem.
Yes, we have to anticipate not only the MOF's machinations, but meddling by politicians too.
appreciate hearing of your bank's intentions, Mr. Furuichi...
We're grateful for your willingness to shoulder the risks in this undertaking...
However, there are still a number of factors that must be considered.
Before doing something as drastic as shutting down a bank—
even a mutual savings bank beset with troubles like this one —
......
we have to be 100% certain the Minister
is ready to go ahead with it, considering the repercussions that are bound to occur.
Our bank would not even consider this undertaking if we were not determined to help prevent a credit collapse.

EXCHANGE: The settlement of debts and credits between distant locations without a direct transfer of currency. Domestic exchange refers to transactions within one country, and foreign exchange to transactions between countries.

All we ask is that you give us the first opportunity to assist your Ministry
in implementing your decision when the time comes.
Yes?
It's not quite that simple
That's certainly our intention.
However...
We just have to hope someone doesn't suddenly throw us a curve ball before this thing gets settled...
They must be in an utter panic at Taigen. If this process bogs down and there's a run on the bank,
it could hurt the credit system of the entire country!
Well, if that happened, it'd be the MOF's own fault!
And there'd be no cushy job in the private sector waiting for the Banking Bureau chief.
Trust me,they're just waiting for the right opportunity.

Sure is taking them a long time.
Yeah, they should've wrapped it up by now.
......
You see, we've heard from other quarters as well...
Even the financial sector is experiencing pressures from overseas these days...
Upstarts who don't know their place, you might say.
......?!
Of course, we intend to give top priority to a Japanese bank — but it wouldn't look right to ignore all other options...
Heh heh ... I'm speaking strictly in the abstract, you understand!
SPLASH

LIQUID DEPOSITS: Deposits used by businesses or individuals for temporarily depositing money, including current deposits (e.g. checking accounts), ordinary and special deposits, deposits at notice, and deposits for taxes. Interest on liquid deposits is low; current deposits pay no interest.

Kyoto: the
Higashiyama
district

The residence of Soichiro Funaoka
You've turned into quite a beautiful young lady since we saw you last, Sawako!
And to think you've made such a success of yourself in America, too!
Please, you're embarrassing me, Mrs. Funaoka! I hardly qualify as successful!

TIME DEPOSITS: Deposits for which the term of the deposit is set in advance and withdrawals technically cannot be made until the term is up. Interest is paid at a higher rate than for liquid deposits; normally the longer the term, the higher the rate.

But it *is* easier for a woman to get ahead in America
than it is in Japan...
When you came here after getting your M.B.A.
and told me you wanted to work in the States ,
that's exactly why I approved of the idea...
......
I gather your work over there didn't even have anything to do with Japan ...
So what brings you back home ?
Companies here wouldn't know what to do with a female M.B.A.!
Yes, that was a policy of Chairman Miller's.
Manhattan Trust hires people of many backgrounds.
Asians, Latinos, what have you — not just white Americans.
And they deliberately give people assignments unrelated to their background
to build up a staff that can work anywhere, is the idea.
So in my case

CREDIT CREATING FUNCTION: A process by which banks create deposits at many times the value of the deposits initially received by lending that money, thereby generating more deposits, which can be used for more loans, in a repeating cycle.

my longest assignment was handling loans to Latin American governments.
I had my hands full with the debt crisis in that region...
I see. So why are you in Japan?
Well, the truth of the matter is
Manhattan Trust was involved in a bit of trouble three years ago.
Yes, I heard! It rated a few inches in the Japanese papers.
The "Edmond Scandal," am I right?
Something about improper exchange dealings, as I recall...
Yes, an employee named Edmond blew the whistle on illegal exchange transactions by the bank.
The financial revolution moved so fast in the U.S. — there were incredible advances in exchange transaction techniques, along with everything else!
People could take advantage of markets around the world, open 24 hours a day...
Techniques for profiting from exchange speculation were actively encouraged at our bank, too...
Rob Peter to pay Paul, and cook your books to cover your tracks, eh?
Oh, Professor!

Actually, there are a lot of complicated tricks involved ...
Well, a detailed explanation would be wasted on me.
The upshot of it is, they went too far, right?
In some cases, it turned out they had violated SEC* regulations
as well as the laws governing exchange transactions.
Too caught up in the money game, eh!
It's just as true of Japan as it is of the U.S.A.
I've said it over and over, but no one listens! The financial sector's addiction
BZZZ...
to meaningless money games could ruin this country!
Calm down, dear!
—and listen to what Sawako has to say!
These idiots are blinded by the gleam of the money they see in front of them, without a thought for the disaster they're creating!
You're absolutely right, Professor!
Manhattan Trust profited handsomely from its exchange dealings...

But Edmond was troubled by the bank's methods.
He first took his concerns to management...
But the top brass thought he was trying to blackmail them, and showed him the door, right?
So Edmond told his story to the SEC...
Yes, and that led to hearings in the U.S. Senate.
In the end, the bank had to admit several instances of wrongdoing
and pay a gigantic fine!
... not to mention the huge sums they spent trying to curry favor with Congress.
Trying to hush things up by paying off the pols, eh...
The same old story, wherever you go!
Still, I think the bank learned its lesson from the experience...

* SEC: The Securities and Exchange Commission of the United States, established in 1934 by the Securities and Exchange Act as an independent body to oversee the administration of securities transactions and accounting practices.

It learned that despite all this talk about financial revolution, the bottom line is the welfare of the individual depositor.
A bank that takes its depositors for granted may do well in the short run, but it won't survive for long! That 's why the current chairman
got picked for the job—he comes from a consumer banking background.
He's been reforming the bank from within
and pushing it in the direction of retail banking.
As you're well aware, Professor, Japanese households have the highest rate of savings
in the entire world!
Hmph! So they finally recognized the obvious, did they!
Now tell me—what does all this have to do with your return to Japan?
Getting its hands on even a fraction of those savings would be great business for any bank!
But meanwhile, credit cards have yet to really catch on in Japan.
If we package a wide range of financial services with credit card accounts, they should spread like wildfire!

My assignment is to develop these personalized services and offer the consumer something Japanese banks don't have...
Sounds like a big job, all right.
But remember, that old pay-as-you-go, packrat mentality is the key to living the good life in Japan!
I'd hate to see you mess things up by importing some crazy American system!
I hear America's full of morons who spend themselves into bankruptcy with credit cards.
... You never were one to mince words, were you, Professor!
When I heard you'd resigned from all those government advisory councils
I was afraid maybe you'd lost some of your fight—but I can see I needn't have worried!
Isn't he the worst old curmu-dgeon?
And remember, I have to put up with this every day!
Take it from me, Sawako—choose your own husband carefully!
Speaking of which, made any progress on that front, young lady?

"COLLATERALISM": The traditional Japanese financial practice of requiring security for money borrowed, bonds issued, etc. By contrast, financial transactions in the U.S. and Europe are often unsecured.

Oh, I don't even have time to think about such things!
Guess you're too busy for an occasional date with me, then!
Ministry of Finance

NO TAXIS BEYOND THIS POINT
Banking Bureau
Mr. Homma—
Even though we graduated from different universities, we're fellow alumni of the Professor Funaoka school, you might say.
So I hope you'll forgive me for coming to you with a rather blunt question.
......

REGULATED/UNREGULATED INTEREST RATES: Regulated interest rates are those based on the official discount rate, including deposit interest rates and prime rates. Unregulated rates are those affected by market trends, such as CD rates and yields on corporate and public bonds.

When our bank's president met with the director of your Banking Bureau the other day,
I understand the director told him another bank
had also offered to purchase Taigen Mutual.
Is that true?
That's precisely why I came to you!
You're privy to all the information flowing through the Ministry.
Look, Mr. Okada.
I'm only in charge of the Investigative Section of the Minister's Secretariat.
Our president says he was led to believe the bank in question is a foreign bank!
Don't you think the bureau chief was most likely speaking in generalities?
After all, Mr. Okada—
your own bank has taken over banks in England and the U.S., hasn't it?
......

It's a little too late to start telling foreign banks here they can't do what Japanese banks do overseas!
Tokyo's offshore market* is already growing by leaps and bounds...
So the rumors are true, are they?
All he's saying is that the Tokyo financial market is already more globalized than anyone could have predicted.
Consequently, it wouldn't be at all surprising if a foreign bank *did* express interest in Taigen...
There you go, jumping the gun again!
Heh heh! If you're so worried about it, why don't you ask Manhattan Trust directly?
Is that bank
Manhattan Trust?

* OFFSHORE MARKET: Market that provides tax, foreign exchange, and other incentives that allow nonresident financial institutions or businesses to procure and utilize funds under favorable conditions. Tokyo, London, New York, and Singapore are examples of offshore markets.

Speaking of Manhattan,
I hear Sawako Matsumoto is back in town.
Yes, I ran into her recently, as a matter of fact.
Hotel Platon, Akasaka, Tokyo

The Japan office of Manhattan Trust boasts a staff of 300, with headquarters in an intelligent highrise in Akasaka. Sawako's office, however, consists of a single room at the nearby Hotel Platon, with only one clerk for staff.
The modest ambience would appear to suggest that Sawako's assignment is equally modest...
Bob? It's me, Sawako.
Can you answer a question for me?
This is purely hypothetical, but...
Suppose someone wanted to acquire Taigen Mutual—what do you think it would cost them?
Whoa! That's one helluva question!
Why, you thinking of buying it?!

No, no!
I was just curious. After all—
everybody in the industry here is speculating about who'll take over Taigen these days!
This wouldn't have something to do with your assignment here, now, would it?!
Aah, never mind.
According to industry rumors, Taigen has 70 billion yen in bad loans that'll have to be written off. If you factor in payroll adjustments, refurbishing branches and so on, I'd guess you're talking 80 billion.
Hmm. That *is* a lot.
Okay, what would it cost to buy land, put up a building from scratch—
and open a new branch in central Tokyo, say?
Well, it's going to vary. I can't just give you a pat answer.
But I hear it cost one bank four billion yen to build a new branch in Ikebukuro.
So Taigen would cost the equivalent of 20 such branches. Sounds like a bargain after all, since Taigen has 53 branches...
I suppose you could say that ...

But not all those branches are paid off, so you can't really calculate their value that easily.
Here we are, both living in Tokyo, and I never get to see you! It's a cryin' shame!
howzabout coming out to play with me?!
Hey, Sawako, instead of playing with numbers,
I know. I just felt like playing with numbers a little.
Fine, Bob, if you're treating!
>Giggle<
The Planning Office of Goyo Bank
A whole month's gone by,
and the MOF still hasn't made up its mind! What's their problem, anyway?!
GOYO BANK

OVER-THE-COUNTER SALE OF GOVERNMENT BONDS BY BANKS: Starting in 1983, banks were allowed to sell Japanese government bonds, previously the exclusive domain of securities firms, in order to increase government bond purchases. This increased the number of sales outlets for these bonds nearly tenfold.

Do they have any viable candidates besides us?
We haven't seen any signs of movement among the other city banks...
Our mole over at Taigen says no one has contacted them directly.
Then what's going on?
Could be some heavy politicking is dragging things out.
Yeah, Taigen's bad debts apparently include a lot of loans to politicians.
Okada, what did you find out about Manhattan Trust?
I've been gathering all the intelligence I can, but it's still not really clear what they're up to.
The woman I mentioned
has been personally checking out branch locations and whatnot...
but there's no indication of contact with the MOF or Taigen.

However, there is one thing that concerns me.
What's that ?
My sources say remittances from Manhattan's headquarters to their Japan office have been increasing lately! They're trying to do it in small increments that won't attract notice, but it's grown to a pretty hefty sum already.
And you think those are purchasing funds, eh?!
Perhaps.
Hmph. Sure sounds like it!
But suppose a foreign bank did buy a Japanese bank—
They'd have a tough time doing business here, wouldn't they?
Well, we run a bank in the U.S., after all...
so we're just talking about a little role-reversal!
Manhattan Trust
was hit with a big scandal a while ago.

LOANS WITH GOVERNMENT BOND COLLATERAL BY SECURITIES FIRMS: To compensate for the newly-approved sale of government bonds by banks, securities companies were allowed to use government bonds as collateral on loans beginning in 1983. These moves further blurred the distinction between the functions of banks and securities firms.

But they've made what many consider a miraculous comeback.
Their strategy may well be based on a point of view totally foreign to ours...
Sure sounds like they could be the reason for the MOF's waffling.
The Prez is starting to get pissed off at our lack of progress on this thing.
GRUMBLE GRUMBLE
If the deal remains stalled, Taigen's depositors will start bailing out,
and the merger's going to look less and less attractive. If we don't play our cards real soon, we may find ourselves stuck with a losing hand.
We've got to attack on both fronts at once— the MOF and Taigen!!
MOF Banking Bureau
I think it's about time, don't you?
No, let's wait another week !
We've got 'em sweating now. If we hold out just a bit longer,
CLIP

we'll have 'em right where we want 'em—
which is between a rock and a hard place...
What about Taigen? Are they following our instructions to the letter?
Taigen's no problem!
They've got 1500 worried employees on their hands...
All right, let's put off the interview Goyo requested for one more week!
CLIP
You'd better make sure the stage is properly set!
CLIP
If everything isn't in order, opening night's gonna be a disaster!
Leave everything to me!
This'll be the most artistic performance you ever saw!
Well, let's not be melodramatic!
HA HA HA HA HA

"HOME BANKING": A system connecting bank computers with terminals in private residences via data communication lines, allowing customers to transfer money, check their account balances, etc. while at home.

Sawako—
I have no idea what your actual assignment is these days...
But let me give you a piece of advice .
Unlike banks in the States, Japanese banks can't lift a finger without the Finance Ministry's permission.
For example-
Banks here hand out free tissue paper packets to their depositors, right?
They can't even do *that* without the blessing of the MOF.
Really!
Well, I'd heard that the primary function of a bank's planning office is to deal with the Finance Ministry.
Right. That's just about all they do.
Every time the bank wants to open a new branch or launch a new service, they have to start wheeling and dealing and kissing up to the MOF!

"FIRM BANKING": A system connecting bank and corporate computers to permit online banking transactions. The use of data communications to perform such transactions is broadly referred to as electronic banking.

In other words, the Ministry calls all the shots!
If the MOF doesn't approve of something and you push ahead with it anyway, you're asking for big trouble!
The bureaucrats have all kinds of ways to make life miserable for a bank.
For example, they can decide to turn a routine inspection into the audit from Hell!
Checking for every last little screw-up—minor errors they'd normally wink at.
You hear plenty of stories of bank staffers driven to nervous breakdowns by this treatment!
Really?!
I've heard that at some banks, the sole job of the planning office is to keep the MOF Inspection Department happy.
When the inspectors arrive, the bank has its prettiest female clerks ready to wait on them hand and foot...
WHAT?!
That's outrageous!!
even sit with them at dinner parties!
Well, one of our people was outraged when a Ministry official told him up front
that we should learn to play ball, too.

Bob!!
Are you saying our bank does the same thing...?!
No, no, of course not!
But you know what they say about "when in Rome"...
and a lot of bureaucrats are unhappy with us for not playing by their rules.
They say we're screwing up the banking system here... heh heh!
Hey, maybe this is what's really behind the financial friction between Japan and the U.S. !
Well, I find it disgusting!
I'm not totally unacquainted with cutthroat competition— but to be forced to engage in sick practices like that—!
It's beyond my comprehension!
You know, Sawako— you really *are* cute when you're angry!
Hmph!!
Anyway, my point is simply that the Finance Ministry is a force you've got to reckon with!
......

INTERNATIONALIZATION OF THE YEN: Defined by the Finance Ministry as the increased use or holding of yen for international transactions — in other words, the rise in the percentage of trade payments, overseas loans, and foreign investment reserves using yen.

Sawako's office
Sorry to drop in like this on such short notice—
but I have something I must ask you!
Oh my! You sound so formal—
now you've got me worried!
......
I know you're very busy, so I'll get right to the point.
Did you return to Japan to oversee the takeover of Taigen Mutual?!
What?!
I've been watching your activities from a distance ...
and it looks to me like you're zeroing in on Taigen.
Hiroshi!
Have you been tailing me?!

I'd heard that planning offices sometimes have to get their hands dirty-but I can't believe you'd —!
Look, the Taigen situation is the number one concern for our bank right now!
It's my duty to check up on any activities we think are a threat to us!
So how about it— are you going to give me a straight answer?!
I have nothing to say to you on that subject, Hiroshi!
If that's what you came for, you may as well leave now !
I'm disappointed — I thought you were more of a gentleman than that!
You always were tough, Sawako.
Fine, I'll leave you with a word of advice.
......
If you think you can force your way into the banking business in Japan
just by taking over an existing bank, you're sadly mistaken!
The Japanese financial world is bound together by a web of personal relationships!
A moment ago you said the Planning Office does dirty work...
Listen, if we weren't out there doing whatever it takes to outwit the MOF, our bank wouldn't be in business for long!

DEREGULATION OF INTEREST RATES: The lifting of restrictions on interest rates imposed by a government or central bank, allowing rates to be freely determined by market forces. The Finance Ministry took its first step in this direction in 1985 by deregulating interest rates on deposits over one billion yen.

You're right, we do play dirty!
When a Ministry inspector shows up, we surround him with pretty girls from the secretarial pool!
Are you ready to do that kind of work yourself?!
Your M.B.A. means nothing in the Japanese business world!
......
If you *did* come back here to buy Taigen,
you may as well give up now!!
Thank you for your generous advice, Hiroshi!
I'll give it careful conside-ration, I can assure you.
Damn—blew it again!!
SLAM

Office of the President Of Goyo Bank
What's going on, Tozaki?
Ever since Taigen's unsound practices came to light, I thought the Finance Ministry was all for forcing them to merge with us !
Now everything's come to a standstill ! What seems to be the problem?
Um, we see no indication that the Ministry's basic attitude has changed...
but for the moment we're at a loss to explain this delay.
What about the rumor that Manhattan Trust has made an offer, and the MOF is trying to figure out how to respond?
Well, we've looked into that but haven't been able to confirm anything.
However, the probability seems slight...
Meanwhile, the whole world now knows what terrible shape Taigen is in!
If the depositors panic and there's a run on Taigen, it'll tarnish our reputation too!
The pundits are saying the old convoy* system won't work anymore!

* "CONVOY" SYSTEM: The Japanese practice of adjusting financial policy to keep the weakest of the nation's financial institutions in business, much as a wartime convoy adjusts to the speed of the slowest ship in the group.

Unless we can acquire Taigen while it's still got some life in it, it's not worth the trouble!
I agree, sir. We need to resolve things in the next day or two.
We're working on the Ministry right now with that objective...
Well, try to make it happen!
We have branches we need but can't open until we know whether this merger's going through!
New York

The U.S. office of Goyo Bank
Rumors are rampant here that Manhattan Trust is trying to take over a Japanese bank...
That's right, Chairman Miller has denied it...
but everybody's talking about it here.
The MOF attache* at the Japanese Embassy
says he's heard no official word to that effect, but..
NIKKEI TELECOM

* ATTACHE: A person with special duties, such as information gathering, assigned to a foreign embassy staff by a government ministry or agency.

Ministry of Finance
......!!

......
BEEP
BEEP
BEEP
I was called here with Mr. McCovey, the president of our Japan office, by the Banking Bureau chief.
It turned out to be just a lot of talk...
But I thought, as long as I'm here,
it'd be nice to see my old classmate, Homma-san!

G5: Abbreviation for the Group of Five, a conference of the finance ministers and central bank governors of Japan, the U.S., England, France, and Germany. The rapid rise of the yen began after a decision to revise the dollar exchange rate at a New York meeting of the G5 in September 1985. [The group became the G7 in 1986 with the inclusion of Canada and Italy — Ed.]

Well, the pleasure is mine, Sawako.
I've heard all about your success in America.
You've been described as Chairman Miller's secret weapon!
To rise to the position of senior economist at your young age would be a feat even for an American!
Oh, it doesn't really count for much.
Anyway, I've heard much grander things about you!
I paid a visit to Professor Funaoka not too long ago...
Oh, the Professor?
Ha ha ha! Knowing him, I bet he called me a few names !
Hardly!
He called you a real straight shooter, for a bureaucrat!
"For a bureaucrat," eh?
HA HA HA
That sounds just like the Professor, all right !

Homma's trying his damnedest to restore the nation's fiscal balance under extremely dire conditions.
But at the same time, he can't ignore the public's need for government services.
Anyway, he's one of the few MOF bureaucrats who'll give you an honest answer.
A real straight shooter, that Homma...
In fact, you ought to pay him a visit.
Actually...
Here you are, sir.
I, um, had a complaint I wanted to share with you.
A complaint?
That doesn't sound like you, Sawako!
It's about something
I wasn't aware of until I started working here in Japan.
I'm astonished at the degree of control exercised by the Finance Ministry

FEDERAL RESERVE BOARD (FRB): Commonly called "the Fed," the administrative organ of the Federal Reserve System of the United States, which functions as a central bank. The Fed determines national monetary policy and supervises the Federal Reserve Banks and their member banks.

over Japan's banking industry... I'd heard the government had adopted a new policy of "liberalization" vis-a-vis the banks.
But compared to America, it seems like you can't pick up your chopsticks here without permission from the authorities!
Our banking system is the last bastion of the economic controls of the war years and the Occupation, you see.
Hmm. I suppose so...
By controlling the flow of money, the government can control the nation's entire industrial structure.
Of course, there's also a legitimate need to protect depositors...
But businesses should be allowed to operate freely as a matter of principle! And as for protecting the depositors, shouldn't that be their own responsibility?
I can't help thinking
that "protecting the depositor" is just a cover for the bureaucrats' efforts to protect their own vested interests!

That's pretty strong medicine you're dishing out, Sawako!
I can't argue with you on that point...
But you should know that many Ministry officials share the opinion that overprotective policies are hazardous to the health of Japan's banks.
I include myself among them. However...
Yes?
Well, in the case of Taigen Mutual, it's clear the bank's management had no ethical scruples whatsoever.
So many of us question whether it would be such a good idea to let them do as they please.
And it's said that Taigen is only the tip of the iceberg — there are many more banks in the same predicament because of their irresponsible lending practices!
Hmph! In the U.S., a bank like that would simply go belly-up!
What I find hardest to accept is this policy of never allowing banks to fail!

MONEY SUPPLY: The outstanding amount of currency and deposits held by the private sector, exclusive of financial institutions. This is generally represented by three indexes, M1, M2, and M3, which are published by the Bank of Japan every month.

You may be right. Maybe we should let at least one bank fail — that might shock the others into mending their ways!
Trouble is, if we do that, we'll be accused of not exercising proper oversight...
But it seems to me you'll have to cross that bridge someday
if Japan's banking industry is ever going to learn to stand on its own two feet!
... I completely agree with you, Sawako.
In fact, the time may come sooner than we think!
Well, when it does, it may be the first real step toward the internationalization of Japanese banking.
That sounds less like a complaint than a non-negotiable demand!
Ha ha ha!
Oh dear! I must sound incredibly arrogant...
Not at all! I enjoy hearing someone voice a frank opinion for a change!

Well, thank you for the opportunity! You know, I feel much better for having talked to you ..
Well, feel free to drop in on your old classmate any time!
Planning Office, Goyo Bank
But now it seems the fruit may fall into someone else's lap if we don't act fast!
That's been our strategy so far.
"Wait for the ripened fruit to fall into your hands..."
We're at the point where our only option is to shinny up the tree and pluck it ourselves.
Yes, we don't have much choice...
We'd better contact our allies in the Diet right away!
It'll cost us, but it's this or nothing...
......

MONEY SUPPLY DEFINITIONS: M1 comprises currency plus demand deposits (e.g. checking accounts); M2 comprises M1 plus time deposits; and M3 comprises M2 plus other deposits and savings (which in Japan includes postal savings, agricultural cooperative deposits, and so on).

MOF Banking Bureau
銀行局
Well, if you're that committed to it, Mr.Furuichi,
perhaps we should entrust Taigen to your care!
If Goyo Bank is willing to merge with Taigen, that eliminates our fears of credit instability with one stroke.
And that will be a great relief to the entire financial sector...
I'm very happy to hear you say that!
Then, may we begin talks with Taigen immediately to expedite the merger?
There are many things we need to look into beforehand...
Of course! You can't have a successful marriage unless you know all about your prospective mate!
But I should warn you, Mr. Furuichi!
We can't have the groom cancelling the wedding once he catches a glimpse of the bride naked!

Taigen Mutual
Savings Bank
headquarters

MONEY SUPPLY ADMINISTRATION POLICY: Control of the growth of the money supply by means which include setting a target or range for the rate of increase in the money supply. This practice began in 1970 when the U.S. Federal Reserve Board publicly announced a target growth rate for the first time.

What's going on?
People from Goyo Bank
are coming to look at our books!
They say Goyo's sending several staffers over to work here.
Why? Is this going to take more than one day?
Sounds like it. I hear two girls from General Affairs are being assigned to wait on them the whole time...
If this merger goes through...
That'll make us employees of Goyo, right?
Wonder if we'll get a raise?
I wouldn't get your hopes up if I were you!
Goyo's known for its tough, bottom-line management.
You can bet the pressure's gonna be on!

Goyo's going to place its own people in charge here, did you hear?
Gawd, I hope I don't have to work under a total stranger!
Never mind that, what's going to happen to our guys in management?
I'd sure hate being stuck at the bottom of the ladder for the rest of my career!
Hey, that could happen to your boyfriend, you know!
If it does, I'll dump him for a Goyo guy!
Oooh, that's cold!!
Planning Office, Goyo Bank

BONDS: Generic term for national government bonds, local government bonds, government-guaranteed bonds, electric utility bonds, general corporate bonds, and yen-denominated bonds issued in Japan by foreign governments or corporations. Local bonds are purchased in 10,000 yen units, national bonds 50,000 yen, and other bonds 100,000 yen.

We've been completely had by the MOF!!
They never let on things were this bad...
I had no idea Taigen's owners were this out of line!
They were obviously waiting for us to panic!!
And even our own investigations failed to reveal
how much worse the actual figures were
than the data they showed us!!

Dammit! It's just not right for the Ministry to take things this far without telling us the whole story!!
BAM
They knew if they showed us all these figures and then asked us to make up our mind,
we'd most likely say no, thanks!
So this was what the MOF meant when it told President Furuichi it wouldn't let
the groom cancel the wedding after viewing the bride naked...!
If we did that, Taigen would go bust for sure —
And our bank would be blamed for it!
Shit! I wish we could wipe the whole damn slate clean!
We've been sold a goddam lemon!
But it's our own fault for falling for some cheap bureaucratic con game!
It'll take us five years, minimum, to recoup the costs of this merger.
And we just have to hope and pray nothing happens that adds to those costs in the meantime!
Do you suppose they were just bluffing about Manhattan Trust too?

REAGAN'S HIGH INTEREST RATE POLICY: Under the banner of "a strong America and a strong dollar," the United States raised interest rates sharply in 1981, thereby strengthening the dollar and increasing the U.S. trade deficit.

This is one helluva June bride we're stuck with!
......
Sawako's office
......
I thought it was odd
when the Finance Ministry suddenly called our branch president in...
as bait so they could reel in Goyo!
Now it looks like we were just being used
......
Those rumors that were flying around New York
must have been the MOF's handiwork too...
Even Hiroshi Okada

was completely taken in by the bureaucrats ...
Tokyo is as cutthroat as any other financial capital!
I'd better keep my eyes open!

Listen, Sawako...
I was convinced you'd returned here to buy Taigen, too!
You must be kidding. My work here is nothing as exciting as that!

KEY CURRENCY: Currency of a particular nation held by other nations in reserve for foreign investment or used for trade payments. The American dollar is no longer the only key currency in the world, as the use of the Deutschmark and the yen continues to grow.

My assignment is to find a bank that will serve as a good partner
with whom we can develop and market personal banking services and new products!
That's all!
Well, I'll be doggone..
That's why I've been checking out a number of different banks.
I'd heardJapan's bureaucrats were clever, but I had no idea they were so downright diabolical!
Those are some scary bastards ...!
Right now, in the name of financial deregulation, they're lowering the old barriers
between banks and securities firms, and between long-term and short-term financing.*
...And the MOF exploited your activities to its advantage! I get it!
Competition is getting fiercer by the day!
Some wags are calling it the Warring Banks Era...
No kidding! And conspiracies are a dime a dozen in wartime, aren't they!

* LONG-TERM/SHORT-TERM FINANCING: In Japan a distinction is made between institutions specializing in long-term financing and ordinary banks primarily engaged in short-term financing. This tradition, known as "long-short segmentation," has recently been challenged as an outmoded practice.

Looks like it's only going to get tougher
to do business in Tokyo, doesn't it.
So it seems.
I just finished reading Sun Tzu's "Art of War"!
If it does, you can count on me!
In that case, I guess I should read "Macbeth"!
HA
HA
HA
HA

HOTEL PLATON

2-1, KIOI-CHO, CHIYODA-KU
TOKYO, JAPAN
PHONE : 03-379-5459

May 29, 1984: This date may well be recorded in economics textbooks as the day Japan's financial system closed the door on the era of restrictions and exclusionism, and entered a new age of liberalization and internationalism. I say this because two documents released on this day altered the course of Japanese banking. One was a report by the Japan-U.S. Yen-Dollar Commission; the other was a Finance Ministry publication titled "The Current Situation and Outlook for the Deregulation of Finance and the Internationalization of the Yen." Together these documents addressed the necessity of converting from the government-controlled financial system of the past forty years to a more liberal structure, and outlined specific steps for achieving this.

Fig. 6-2 Changes in the Current Value of Public and Corporate Bon

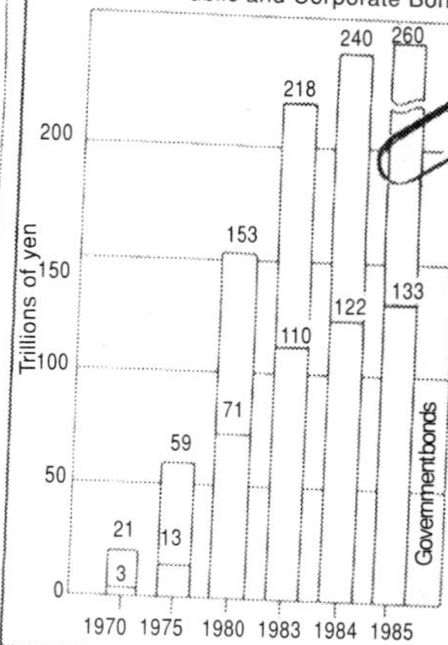

The two main recommendations of these reports were: (A) the phased deregulation of deposit interest rates, and (B) the easing of restrictions on foreign banks. As a result, foreign banks like ours were offered the same benefits in Japan that Japanese banks already enjoy in America -- which is why there are suddenly fears here that Manhattan Trust will try to acquire Taigen, and so on. But interest rate deregulation was extended only to wholesale banking, and the Finance Ministry's "guidance" of the banks remains oppressive. So it's really too early to say that deregulation and internationalization have been achieved. Still, Japan's financial sector is likely to undergo some dramatic changes over the next few years.

Table 6-4 Steps Toward Financial Deregulation and Internationalization

gulation: Deposit interest rates
- Reduce minimum unit for CDs (300 million → 100 million yen)
- Reduce minimum term for CDs (3 months → 1 month)
- Permit handling of new large-denomination money market certificates
- Deregulate large deposit interest rates
- Deregulate small deposit interest rates

blish yen-denominated bank acceptance market

nationalization: Entry of foreign financial institutions into Japan
- oreign banks enter trust business
- oreign banks deal in government bonds
- n up Tokyo Stock Exchange membership

:Internationalization of the yen
- ralize the European market
- ban on short-term lending to residents
- nit issuance of Euroyen CDs
- x restrictions on issuance of Euroyen bonds onresidents
- ish restrictions on yen-dollar swapping
- pt more flexible rules on issuance of yen-omination foreign bonds

② Car Wars

"The logic of private enterprise is predicated entirely upon vigorous competition in a free market. The encouragement of competition and the perpetuation of a free market are vital to the maintenance of a system of private enterprise."—Cartel and Monopoly Commission of the Twentieth Century Fund

BZZZZZZ BZZZZZ
BZZZZZZ BZZZZZ
......
BZZZZZ BZZZZ

The Funaoka residence
You were born in Wakayama prefecture, weren't you, my dear?
Yes, in Shingu. Why?
TINKLE
Your great-grandpa belonged to the Soma Clan
and was a member of the Iwakura Mission, right?
Yes, he made a grand tour of America and Europe—
he even stayed on in Germany and studied medicine there, I'm told.
...Which makes him one of the first Japanese to study abroad!

DOMESTIC MARKETING PLAN: Japan's top five automakers announced plans to increase their 1987 domestic sales by 4.1% over 1986, while reducing exports by 1.7% — a sign of the intense domestic competition brought on by the rising yen's eradication of export profits.

Then your granddad was a doctor with the Navy
And your daddy runs his own clinic back home, am I right?
So you come from a long line of doctors...
???
Why are you bringing this up, Professor?
Oh, I was just wondering why Manhattan Trust made you a senior economist so quick, and then vice-president of their Japan office to boot!
Ha ha ha!
What are you saying, dear?! Sawako earned those positions on her own merits and you know it!
That's all right! You know the title of vice-president doesn't count for much in America!
It's like being a division manager in Japan...
Now look, I wasn't questioning Sawako's ability...
After all, she graduated from Kyoto, and I was her teacher! If anyone knows she's got talent, it's me!
Hmph!
But think about it—you've got the biggest bank in America,
chock full of people with "talent" all climbing the same ladder...
Well, even so, how many women as young as you are become vice-presidents?!

in a business environment dominated by the American philosophy of efficiency above all else.
And you were able to break out of the pack in a place like that... which leads me to believe there's something different about you.
Something different?!
I don't mean because you were an Asian in America. I'm talking about the reverence for life you acquired growing up in a doctor's house-hold— in other words, your warm heart!
I see your point. I guess a warm heart *would* stand out in the cold world of banking!
Um, excuse me...
?!
That's what I was talking about.
Why, it's Mr. Suzuki!
What a surprise! Do come in!
I just happened to be in the neighborhood...
Then I remembered the Professor lived around here, and I couldn't resist dropping by... I hope I'm not imposing.

AUTO SALES: Under the Japanese system, auto dealers sell only their parent company's products, engaging in direct wholesaling of specific models within a specific territory by agreement among the automakers.

BUZZZ BUZZZ BUZZZ BUZZZ
What's the matter, son?
You look tired! What are you up to these days?
Well, I switched jobs not long ago— I'm in auto sales now.
It's tough work, and I'm still getting used to it... I'm completely bushed.
Sales!
That sounds like a terrible waste of a talented engineer like you!
Well, until recently I was working as a design team leader
at the Hiroshima plant of Matsudai Motors...
But then they decided to cut production, so they transferred me to their dealership here. Now I'm a salesman.
Trouble is, I'm no good at it— I haven't sold a single car in three months.
Don't blame yourself!
Toyote Motors has a powerful sales network in these parts!

When Toyote set up its dealerships here way back when,
they aggressively courted the local movers and shakers. That gave 'em a rock-solid "in" with the community.
Well, our dealers are directly under the thumb of the home office...
So, everyone's always looking over his shoulder at headquarters. None of our staff has really put down any roots locally.
But the salesmen over at Toyote are all pros at this game...
Exactly! They make the rounds of the local Chamber of Commerce, trade associations, neighborhood groups, the PTA...
High school and college alumni groups, hobby clubs, you name it...
They make every contact they can, and carefully nurture 'em all!
Of course, they've been at it for ten or twenty years now!
I know, I know... Rome wasn't built in a day...
The common wisdom is that marketing clout is directly proportional to the size of your sales force.
But there's more to it than that.
It's the skill of your sales reps that separates the winners from the losers...
Toyote and Nissin have a price cushion of about 100 thousand yen per car...
That's much bigger than our margin.

DEALER NETWORK: Japan has 1,800 dealerships affiliated with 11 automakers and boasting 14,700 sales offices and 330,000 employees. Of these, 110,000 are sales reps who sell around 3.1 million passenger cars and 2.5 million commercial vehicles every year.

So we're never in the running in any kind of price war...
All the Japanese automakers grew fat at the trough of the American market—but the high yen put an end to all that, didn't it!
That's why they have to make their cars in the U.S., and meanwhile try to grab a bigger share of the domestic market here!
So the Car Wars are escalating
in both the U.S. and Japan, eh...
Yep, it's hell if you go to America
and hell if you stay in Japan!
January 29, 1986...
"Hell"...!

Stuttgart, West Germany:
The executives of the world's auto companies meet at Leueschloss Castle to celebrate the "100th Birthday of the Automobile."
One hundred years ago today—

WORLD'S FIRST CAR: In January 1886, Karl Benz obtained a patent on a three-wheel automobile with a four-cycle gasoline engine; its top speed was only ten miles per hour. Benz put his car on the market that same summer.

Karl Benz, often referred to as the Father of the Automobile,
obtained a patent for the manufacture of the world's first motorcar...
We have invited representatives from automakers around the world to gather here today
to celebrate this centennial with us. Our company is extremely honored by your presence.

GERMAN AUTO INDUSTRY: Before World War II, the Daimler-Benz Co. alone produced as many cars as Japan's entire auto industry. In 1985, however, West Germany produced only 4.4 million vehicles, less than half Japan's output.

As we look back tonight on a century during which the automobile has vastly improved our quality of life,
let us also look ahead, and vow together to make even better cars in the future!
CLAP
CLAP
CLAP
CLAP
CLAP
CLAP
CLAP
CLAP
CLAP
CLAP
CLAP
CLAP
Hmph!
...And now, let's turn the dance floor over to the swinging sounds of the Mello Tones...
Miss Matsumoto!

You've always looked charming in a kimono, my dear —but that Mandarin dress really becomes you!
You'll agree to one dance to make an old man happy, won't you?
With pleasure!
Nissin Motors Chairman Junichiro Nishihara
Handa Motors Chairman Takashi Okano
Wha-?!
Toyote Motors Chairman Jiro Toyote

GM POWER: Final figures for 1985 showed General Motors passing Exxon to rank no. 1 globally with sales of $96.372 billion -- but in 1986, GM's earnings fell to second place behind Ford's for the first time in 62 years.

Sawako! Sawako Matsumoto, isn't it?
Akio Morikawa! Remember me?
Akio...? From Harvard Business School?
That's me! Your humble under-classman!
Wow, I can't believe it's you! ...So tell me, how does a senior economist at Manhattan Trust wind up dancing with the Chairman of Federal Motors?!
Oh, we go way back — I'm in charge of FM's account at our bank...
No kidding!
I guess that makes us rivals, then, since I work at Toyote!
Yeah, I'm assigned to their U.S. plant now.
I'm just here as part of the Chairman's entourage...
Toyote! Really?!
In charge of the FM account, eh?
Then I guess you must be keeping plenty busy with their Jupiter Project!
The ultimate compact — ready to repel the Japanese invasion with one blow! Scary stuff!
Ha ha! You don't sound very scared, Akio!

SATURN PROJECT: A plan announced by General Motors in 1985 to challenge Japanese compact cars in the U.S. Ford and Chrysler embarked on similar strategies with their Alpha Project and Liberty Project.

In fact, you seem pretty confident of victory!
Not at all. We're quaking in our boots!
So go easy on us, okay, Sawako?!
Akio, look! What's that down there?
Hm?
Oh, those are the bodies of lemmings!
You didn't see them earlier today?
They're native to Norway...
Every four years or so, they leap into rivers or the ocean in a kind of mass suicide.
Mass suicide?! How awful! But why?

GERMAN AUTO INDUSTRY: Before World War II, the Daimler-Benz Co. alone produced as many cars as Japan's entire auto industry. In 1985, however, West Germany produced only 4.4 million vehicles, less than half Japan's output.

Yes—
let's go
back
inside!
No one
knows...
Sure is
creepy,
though.
A toast to 100 years
of the automobile!!

AUTO FRICTION: “As long as we compete in business, there will always be trade friction. Friction disappears only when one side or the other is utterly defeated.” — Eiji Toyoda, Chairman of Toyota Motors

New York
Headquarters of Manhattan Trust
Sawako, please bring the FM file up to the Chairman's office.

FM announced its second-quarter results today.
How do they look?
Well, I just read that FM stock hit a twelve-month low, so as you might guess the figures don't look good.
Sales were up 10.2% over last year, but their net profits are down 18.5%.
And their market share?
It's at 42% — that's four points below what it was five years ago.
FM has invested record amounts in plant and equipment lately, churned out one new model after another —and what good has it done them?!

U.S. MARKET: *Business Week* magazine predicted that in 1990, domestic production by the Big Three would fall to 5.5 million vehicles, less than 80% of current output, while imports would rise to 1.1 million.

Things don't bode well for 1990.
Yep, the Japanese makers' U.S. transplants will be up and running at full throttle by then!
The total supply of autos in the U.S. is now a little under 15 million units, but demand doesn't exceed 12 million.
The hell you say!
Three million cars too many?!
America's besieged now—
not just by Japan and Europe, but Yugoslavia, South Korea, Brazil, Taiwan, Mexico—
35 automakers worldwide, all fighting for a piece of the American pie...
Yep, selling cars in this country was like taking candy from a baby—
and the Big Three had the candy shop all to themselves.
An American car can cost twice as much to make as an import—
and until now, the customer has had to pay the difference.
But then, instead of cutting costs, in 1981 they forced Japan to put "voluntary restraints" on its export of low-priced, high-quality cars...

And those restraints simply raised sticker prices — in effect, they created a U.S.-Japan cartel...
with automakers from both countries conspiring to reap the rewards!
Until the yen's appreciation blew the cartel out of the water.
Right...
When the strong yen eliminated their profit margin on exports, the Japanese makers were forced to start building their cars in the U.S.
And now we have automakers from around the world swarming into the American market in droves...!!
......!!

WORLD CAR PLAN: A strategy implemented by U.S. automakers as they expand into the compact market from their traditional base of fullsize and midsize cars; it includes the globalization of basic designs and the shifting of parts production to low-cost countries.

As FM's bank, I think we need to convey our concern
about these latest figures and the low price of their stock...
I've already arranged for that.
I want you to meet with FM Chairman Adams at his office at 11 a.m. tomorrow!
Yes, sir.

Miss Matsumoto?
Flowers! Who on earth...?
To my charming and delightful upperclass-woman: Would you consent to join me as my guest, not my rival, for the evening? I'll be waiting at the Mövenpick Restaurant at 8 p.m.
Akio Morikawa
Akio!
>GIGGLE<
Senior Economist
Have a nice date!
Thanks—but first I've got to work out a bit!

JAPANESE AUTO PRODUCTION: 1986 output was 12.259 million vehicles— a drop of 0.1% for the first time in four years, due to the strong yen and voluntary restraints on exports to the West. Even so, Japan has produced over 10 million cars a year since 1980, making it the world's top automaking nation.

A toast, then, to the prettiest senior economist anywhere, and to her salary of eighty grand!
Mövenpick Restaurant
You're really pouring on the charm, Akio...
You must have some secret agenda!
Oops, saw through me, didja?
Seriously, though --
Eighty thou's pretty damn good for someone so young!
I guess resumés really do count for something at American firms!

Here I am, a Harvard grad just like you, and Toyote's not paying me a penny more than anyone else they hired the same year!
It's true — nearly everybody in management in this country has a business school background.
There's a clear distinction between management and rank-and-file employees in that respect.
I think Americans are even more obsessed with resumés than the Japanese are!
I gather your company's rushing to move up its schedule for U.S. production,
what with the steep rise in the yen over the past year...
You got it! ... We have a heck of a time getting the American workers at our U.S. plant to accept management Japanese-style.
Well, we can do okay up to about 155 yen to the dollar.
But when it gets stronger than that, it's cheaper for us to make cars locally.
CHOMP CHOMP
For Nissin, the cutoff's more like 170 yen to the dollar...
For Matsudai, it's around 175... Each company has its own break-even exchange rate, you might say.
As long as they could pump the profits from U.S. sales into marketing back home, Japanese automakers were doing just fine.

EFFECT OF THE STRONG YEN: The rise of the yen caused a steeper than expected plunge in Japanese corporate profits. Nissan posted a 19.7 billion yen operating loss at its interim closing in September 1986 — the company's first such loss since it was listed in 1951.

But now each company depends for survival
on its ability to turn a profit in the U.S.!
You're absolutely right! If we only make cars in Japan, we'll wither on the vine. That's why we have no choice but to come to this far-off land and engage in "Car Wars"!!
As you can tell, it's turned me into a raving imperialist overnight!
>GIGGLE<
"The fate of the empire hangs on the U.S. market," eh?
Interesting!
Nice turn of phrase, Sawako!
HA HA HA!
That's why every single maker is strapping on his sword for the Nineties!
Well, you all seem to think you can win. But with a surplus of three million vehicles, somebody's going to get left behind, you know!
The world's automakers are all determined
to jump in the race...
Sounds like building a quality car at even a slightly lower cost
is the key to survival, wouldn't you say?

It's as if an irresistible force, beyond human control,
is driving us all into battle!
Yeah, sometimes it scares me to think about it.
Now wait, we weren't supposed to be rivals tonight, were we!
That's right! ...
So whaddaya say we get outta here, and go dancing someplace?!
Oh dear!
I'm afraid I can't. I have to fly out tomorrow morning to meet with the chairman of Federal Motors!
SLUMP

FIVE-POLE CONFIGURATION: The global auto industry was once described as "tripolar," the poles being Japan, the U.S., and Europe. Now, with the advent of the U.S. compact market, the industry has a five-pole configuration that includes South Korea and Taiwan, as well as Eastern Europe.

Headquarters of Federal Motors
FEDE
The Chairman's office
Our sales are up 10.2% over last year!
We're still number one in the world, so what are you worrying about?!
But look at this year's figures.—

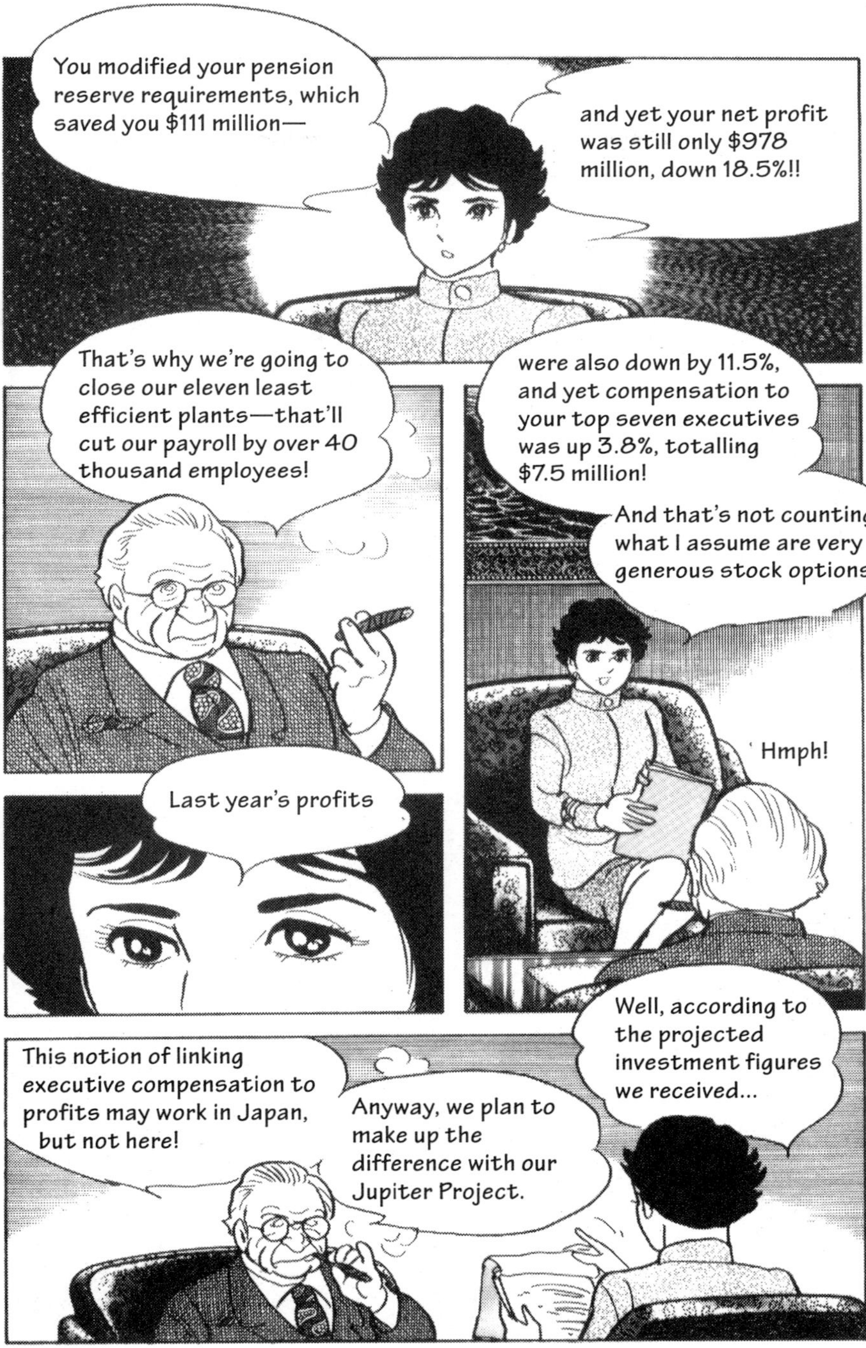

You modified your pension reserve requirements, which saved you $111 million—
and yet your net profit was still only $978 million, down 18.5%!!
That's why we're going to close our eleven least efficient plants—that'll cut our payroll by over 40 thousand employees!
Last year's profits
were also down by 11.5%, and yet compensation to your top seven executives was up 3.8%, totalling $7.5 million!
And that's not counting what I assume are very generous stock options!
Hmph!
This notion of linking executive compensation to profits may work in Japan, but not here!
Anyway, we plan to make up the difference with our Jupiter Project.
Well, according to the projected investment figures we received...

JUST-IN-TIME SYSTEM: The name used by GM when it adopted Toyota's "kanban" system, which aims at minimizing inventory costs by managing deliveries of materials in the proper quantity and timing for immediate use.

You intend to invest $5 billion in the Jupiter Project. That's far too much!
If that's all borrowed money, your annual interest will come to about $500 million.
Now, the best-selling car in the same class as the Jupiter is the Chavo Cavelier, which sells 430 thousand units...
For a car that's supposed to sell for six or seven thousand,
Even if you sold that many Jupiters, you'd still be saddled with nearly $1200 in interest per vehicle!
don't you think that's a bit too much of a competitive handicap?!
You've also provided estimates of labor costs at your Jupiter plant that seem unrealistically low.
You won't be able to convince the UAW* to go along with wages that low!
Leave the UAW to us!
We'll deal with them somehow...
URR
That's not all. FM's inventory as of August was one million vehicles —
that's excessive as well!
After all, your '87 line will be coming out soon...

* UAW: United Auto Workers, America's second largest labor union; it represents aerospace and agricultural workers as well as the auto industry. A powerful voice in Congress, the UAW has been an ardent supporter of the local content bill.

You're always so good at keeping us apprised of the cold hard facts, my dear...
and I truly appreciate your wise counsel!
SNORT...
But you must realize that FM is already gearing up for the battle of the Nineties...
So I suggest you just relax and enjoy the ride!
And now, I have other business to attend to, so I'll have to see you out, little lady!!
......!

Toyote Motors' New York office
What?!
FM is offering auto loans at 2.9%?!
T-that's ridiculous! No one can afford to finance purchases at rates that low!
Guess they've decided to have a fire sale on their '86 inventory—
after all, they're stuck with a million of 'em.
Hmm... This smells to me like
a deliberate strategic move by FM!
Meanwhile, everyone's rushing to establish a toehold here...
Japanese makers are watching their profits plunge as the yen rises...

So now, just when we're staggering under huge investments in new transplant construction...
You hit the nail on the head, Morikawa.
This is a preemptive strike — timed to catch the Japanese while we're hamstrung by the high yen and not yet in battle formation!
Yeah, they know the Japanese makers will have their transplants fully online by 1990. This is an attempt to nip that threat in the bud!
We've gotta stand and fight, boss!!
Toyote makes the least expensive cars in the world!
Bastards!
Do they think we'll just roll over and play dead?!
Hmm... Well, these days,
FM is making the lowest quality cars at the highest cost among the Big Three.
It's like a giant lurching around on his last legs!
So this may be the perfect opportunity for us to launch a frontal attack with the midsize line we've been working on.
They say FM's Jupiter Project isn't going so well, either...

GM-BASHING: At the end of 1986, General Motors Chairman Roger Smith fired Ross Perot, chairman of a GM subsidiary and a critic of GM with a popular following. Perot's crime was to accuse GM strategists of ignoring the consumer and GM management of being excessively bureaucratic.

And they went and fired Poirot, the leader of the reform faction inside FM!
As usual, it's the bean-counters who run the show there.
When they start kicking out the people who really know how to make cars, they're just digging their own graves!
Morikawa, I want you to make the rounds of the dealerships and get some hard data on where we stand. This war's only going to get bloodier!
ssir!
The Board of Directors Room at Toyote's Japan headquarters
Hmph. It's like watching the death throes of a sick elephant...
Perhaps it's time to put the W-50 strategy into action. Time for some hand-to-hand combat!!
Our U.S. sales are in tip-top shape!

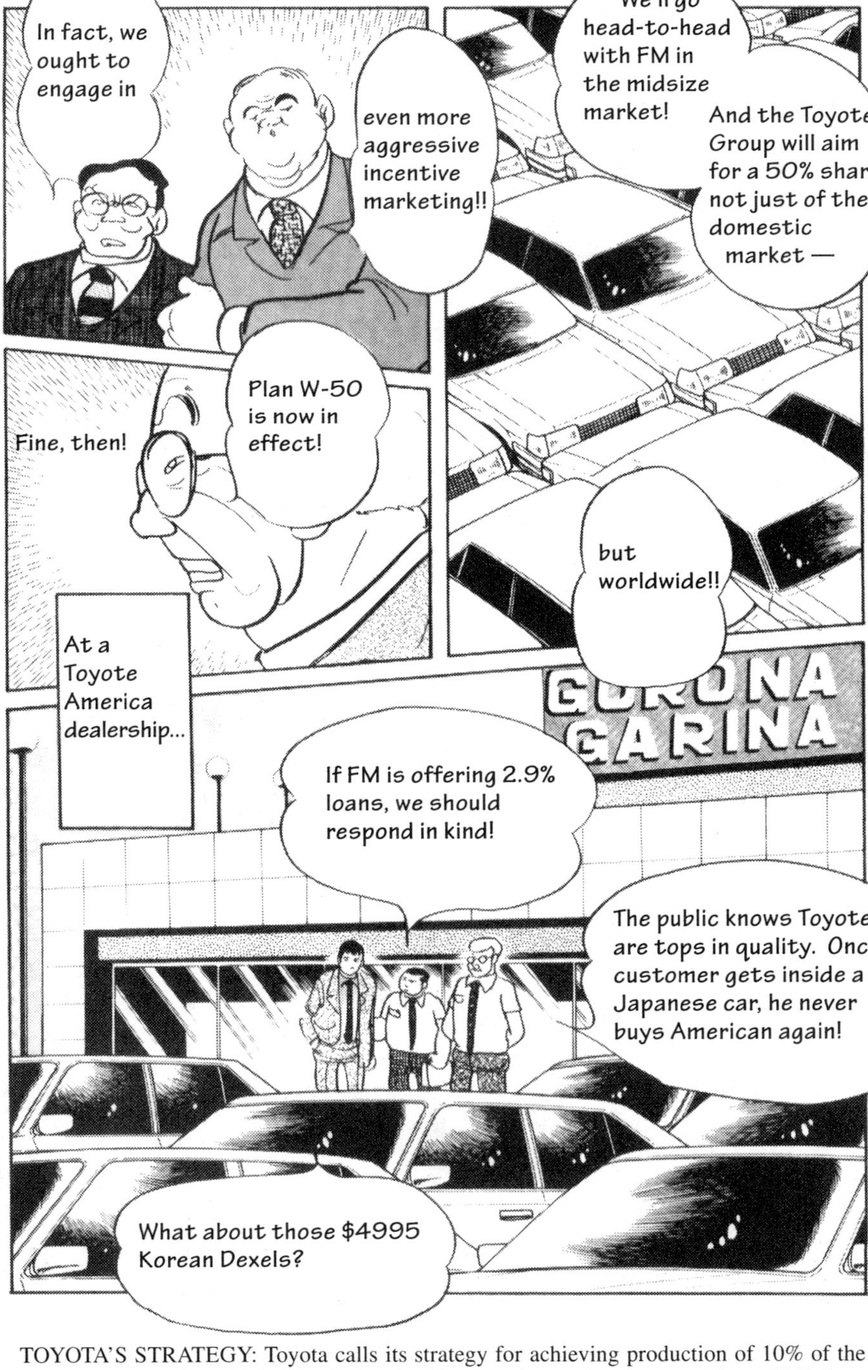

In fact, we ought to engage in
even more aggressive incentive marketing!!
We'll go head-to-head with FM in the midsize market!
And the Toyote Group will aim for a 50% share, not just of the domestic market —
Fine, then!
Plan W-50 is now in effect!
but worldwide!!
At a Toyote America dealership...
GORONA GARINA
If FM is offering 2.9% loans, we should respond in kind!
The public knows Toyotes are tops in quality. Once a customer gets inside a Japanese car, he never buys American again!
What about those $4995 Korean Dexels?

TOYOTA'S STRATEGY: Toyota calls its strategy for achieving production of 10% of the world's automobiles "Global Ten." Another Toyota scheme aimed at acquiring a 50% share of the domestic auto market is known as "T-50."

Their price nosedives once they're used.
In other words, their quality is so high, they depreciate only 2.5%!
Japanese cars, on the other hand, sell for 97.5% of their mint price even after a year!
And those Korean cars don't really come so cheap —most of their customers have to buy 'em at high interest rates!
Why's that?
Over 90% of the people who buy Japanese cars have access to low-interest loans from banks or credit companies.
But half the folks who buy the Korean cars, or those $3990 Guyos, are in the low-income bracket and can't qualify for low interest rates.
So they wind up paying more in the end... I see!
Customers are no fools!
After 1981,
when the voluntary export restraints* kicked in, we added all kinds of options to our cars and raised prices as much as $2000 per unit.
TWINC

* VOLUNTARY EXPORT RESTRAINTS: The Japanese government's policy of maintaining annual passenger car exports at a certain level (2.3 million vehicles as of 1987). Spurred by protectionist pressures within the U.S., these "voluntary" restrictions have been in place since 1981.

And there was already a one or two thou premium on the price before that. It just goes to show how popular Japanese cars are!
Even now, we shouldn't have to worry too much about any difference in price!
And to think, you used to tell me—
Heh!
"If we switch over to local production, the cars will be no good because American blue collar workers are no good...
It's better to keep importing finished products!"
HAHA...
But our U.S.-made cars sell just fine now!
I guess that testifies to the success of Japanese-style business management in America!
Or to the success of joint Japanese-American management!
Yeah, back then I just didn't believe Americans were capable of building cars of the same quality...
Speaking of which, I've got to fly out to our Ohio plant...

Maryhill, Ohio
Toyote's U.S. plant
If we're going to start making midsize cars,
we'll have to build a third production line from scratch!
Besides which we've been holding off on full model changeovers. We'll need to convert our lines for that too...

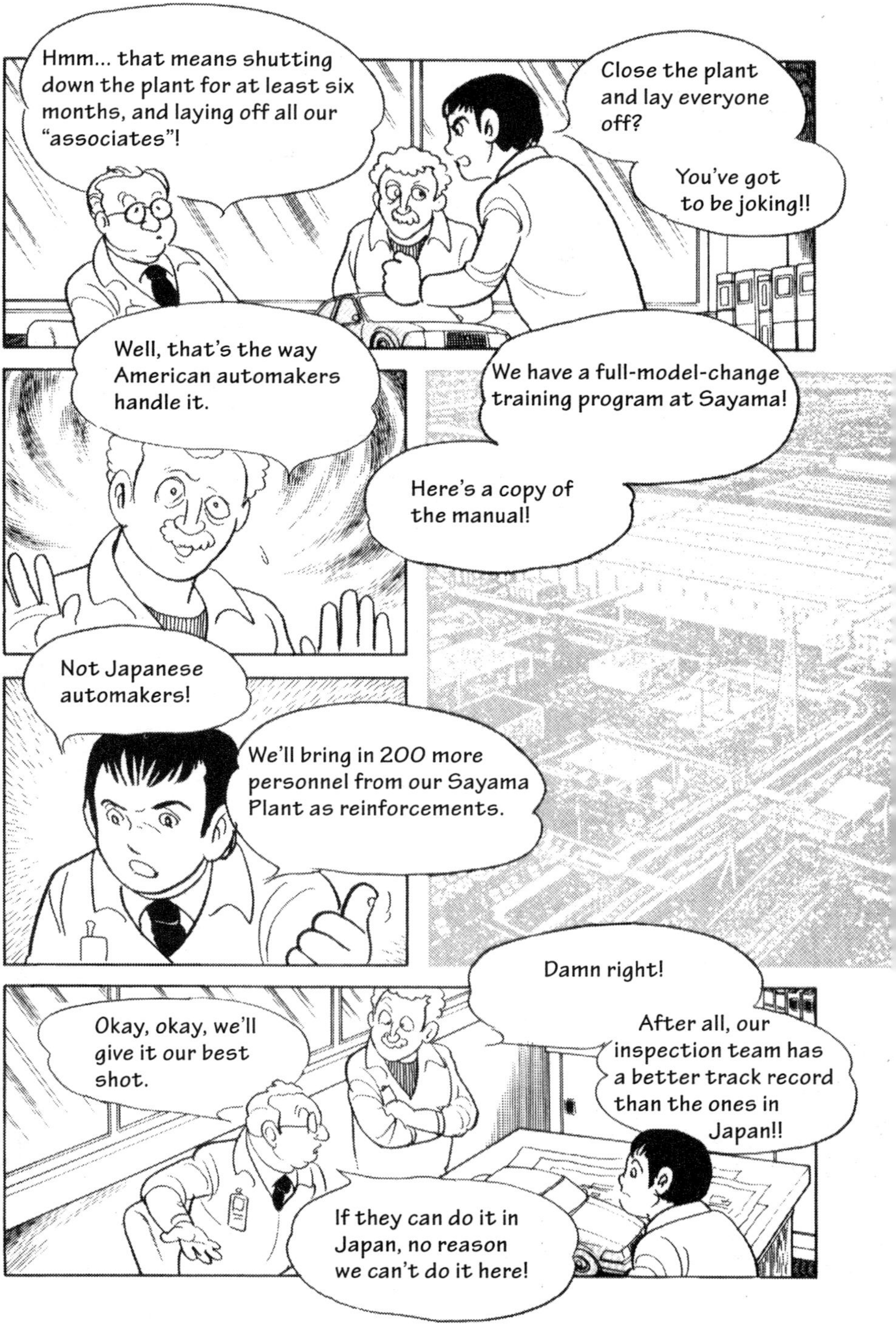

Hmm... that means shutting down the plant for at least six months, and laying off all our "associates"!
Close the plant and lay everyone off?
You've got to be joking!!
Well, that's the way American automakers handle it.
We have a full-model-change training program at Sayama!
Here's a copy of the manual!
Not Japanese automakers!
We'll bring in 200 more personnel from our Sayama Plant as reinforcements.
Okay, okay, we'll give it our best shot.
Damn right!
After all, our inspection team has a better track record than the ones in Japan!!
If they can do it in Japan, no reason we can't do it here!

This'll be the first time an American plant has pulled off a model change without shutting down!!
Hey, this is exciting!!
All for one and one for all!
We're gonna sock it to 'em!!
......
It takes FM three hours to switch dies*, but we only need ten minutes!
No problemo!
Yeah, the Big Three are into low-variety, large-lot production, but we do high-variety, small-lot!
Well, if you're determined to make your money from large-lot production, it makes sense to use heavy, hard-to-move dies like FM does.
But nowadays the public wants variety in their cars.
If you ask me, they'd be better off switching to dies like ours that can be replaced tout-de-suite!
Yeah, our assembly plant, with its computerized robots and kanban** inventory system, is custom-made for high-variety, small-lot output!

* DIE: A metal mold used to stamp sheet steel in the mass production of parts of uniform shape and size. Types of die include stamping, forging, diecast, and plastic dies.

** KANBAN SYSTEM: A system for reducing parts inventory by coordinating parts arrivals with the production process. "Kanban" means signboard, for the signs used to indicate parts quantities and delivery times. Toyota initiated this system, which has spread to other automakers in Japan and, more recently, the U.S. (where it is called "just-in-time").

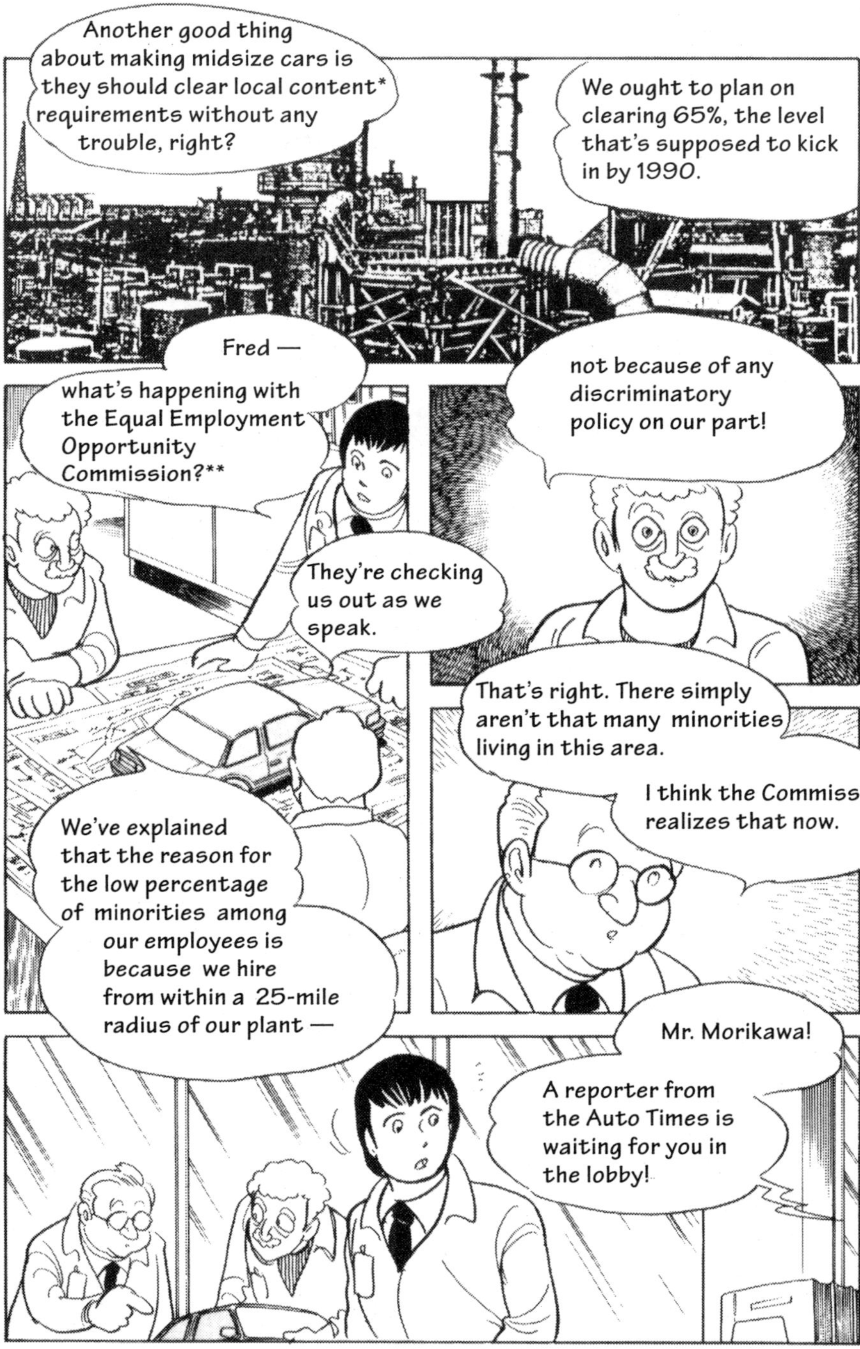
Another good thing about making midsize cars is they should clear local content* requirements without any trouble, right?
We ought to plan on clearing 65%, the level that's supposed to kick in by 1990.
Fred —
what's happening with the Equal Employment Opportunity Commission?**
They're checking us out as we speak.
We've explained that the reason for the low percentage of minorities among our employees is because we hire from within a 25-mile radius of our plant —
not because of any discriminatory policy on our part!
That's right. There simply aren't that many minorities living in this area.
I think the Commission realizes that now.
Mr. Morikawa!
A reporter from the Auto Times is waiting for you in the lobby!

* LOCAL CONTENT LAW: A bill proposed (but never passed) in Congress that would require automakers selling their cars in the U.S. to use U.S.-made parts. The original bill required that domestic parts make up 50% of the wholesale price of a car.

** EQUAL EMPLOYMENT OPPORTUNITY COMMISSION: Monitors businesses in the U.S. to prevent discriminatory hiring practices. The Commission determines if a corporation is hiring minorities in the same ratio they comprise of the local population.

Sawako!! What's the big idea?!
What's this about the Auto Times?
You don't think they'd let me in the door if I told them
>GIGGLE!<
I was in charge of the FM account at Manhattan Trust, do you?
Actually, I was hoping you'd give me a tour of your plant.
Whoa! S-sorry, that's one thing I just can't do!
I mean, you represent our biggest competitor, for God's sake!
Oh, relax!
I just want to learn more about how Japanese-style management works here...
No way!!
Please, Sawako, ask me anything but that!!

Recently I've been thinking it's a shame that, for all my business school background in financial analysis, I really don't know what it's like to manage a business on-site!
And your plant here is considered a model for the rest of the U.S., so I thought maybe...
Noo! Noo! Anything but flattery!!
Of course, I don't expect a tour for free.
So I've brought you a little present!
P-present?!
WHAAA?!
The UAW's president Berby made a secret deal with FM's Adams?!
That's right. I'm told they have a special agreement about the Jupiter Project!
Berby agreed that wages at the Jupiter plant could be 80% of other plants, with the difference made up in profit sharing and bonuses for exceeding targets!
Huh! Those are pretty damn pragmatic concessions for the UAW!
And that's not all. Apparently, the UAW is determined to organize your plant here...

Oh, they are, are they?! A while back, they put an ad in the local paper, accusing management here of being paternalistic and autocratic, urging our employees to vote the UAW in...
But most of 'em voted no, so we thought the union boys had given up. Guess they've decided to take another whack at us, after all!
Well, the UAW
has always pushed for rigidly subdivided job descriptions as a way to increase the number of employees.
But that approach only seems to have turned workers into unthinking robots!
Damn right.
...Who can be fired with impunity!
Now all you have is a bunch of unmotivated, unskilled workers...
Hey, look, Sawako—
I'll give you that guided tour you wanted!
Now you're talking!
I knew you'd see the light!

We pay our workers $12.70 an hour. FM pays $13.70 —
but if you include bonuses, we pay better. And our working conditions are better too!
I want to make sure you see what I mean before you leave here!
So how do I look?
Lovely as ever!
You could wear a sack, Sawako, and you'd still look great!
Now who's flattering whom?!
Can't help it, it's true!
Ha ha ha
...Everyone who works here, manager and worker alike, wears the same uniform.

HONDA'S U.S. PRODUCTION: Honda plans to manufacture engines and transmissions at its Ohio plant with the goal of producing cars that are "100% U.S.-made." By 1990 Honda intended to have two-thirds of the parts in its cars made in the U.S.

We have about 4,000 employees, and we're capable of turning out 300,000 units a year.
We call all of our employees "associates," regardless of rank...
That's right. If a manager gets to the office late, he has to park far away from the building just like everyone else!
I've heard that everyone eats together in the cafeteria and parks in the same parking lot.
And everybody takes their meals here, in the same cafeteria.
There are two shifts, from 6:30 a.m. to 3 p.m., and 4:30 p.m. to 1 a.m.
What are the working hours?
...with a total of 50 minutes for lunch and breaks during each shift.

What sort of meeting is that over there?
It's like QC activities in Japan except we pay overtime for 'em here.
What we call a QC circle activity.*
So do you do pre-shift warmup exercises too, just like in Japanese factories?
Yes, it's a great idea to keep everyone informed about company performance, production targets, and so on.
And what about employee training?
Nope, that's the one thing we didn't import! But we do hold meetings like we do in Japan.
Oh, that goes without saying! We give 'em thorough training in multiple job skills, just as we do in Japan.
Hmm. I guess it's no wonder they're more productive than the workers who get treated like robots by American-style management!
And they're all for it, because they know the more skills they have, the less likely they'll be laid off!

* QC CIRCLE: Workers are organized into small on-site groups to optimize quality control (QC) with the objective of improving day-to-day work procedures and overall productivity.

...So how do you like working at this plant?
A lot better than the last place I was at!
Yeah, people get along fine here...
And the bonuses are a big incentive, too!
The meetings are great — they help you understand the part you're playing inside this huge corporation.
It's great just to know we won't be laid off.
At my old plant, I never once talked to the top brass — but here it's like we're all members of the same community!
I'm glad the UAW isn't here!
We don't need some professional agitator stepping in between us and management!
Everyone tells me the same thing — if they've got to work someplace, they're glad it's here!
Really!

Seeing your plant makes me realize how much Harvard-style management tends to treat people as nothing but "labor providers"...
Yep, it was the Harvard boys who came up with this whole notion of "rational" management for a pluralistic nation like the U.S.
I certainly hope it doesn't catch on in Japan...
Well, thanks for the tour, Akio!
I learned a lot today!
Think nothing of it!
I owe you for that, uh, present you brought!
But you know, we're going to be getting into full-scale production of midsize* cars by the end of the year. That puts us on a head-on collision course with FM!
I know—
although I'm not very optimistic about FM's prospects in that battle!
With everyone turning out more cars, they'll face stiffer competition than ever in the marketplace.
Well,
I guess competition is what business is all about!

* MIDSIZE CAR: Japanese-made midsize cars are slightly larger than compacts. The U.S. market has evolved into a segregated market of American fullsize cars, European midsize cars, and Japanese compacts.

Competition is the engine that improves productivity and raises economic standards...
Hey, they taught us that at Harvard!

So competition is everything, is it...

Wha-?!
Yep, competition is all that counts!
The only way to survive is to come out on top in the marketplace...
......
Everybody's talking about how Ford finally overtook FM as the most profitable automaker in the world.
has its hands full just staying afloat in the Japanese market...
But my company
ZOOOM-

24-HOUR PLANT: GM announced that in the fall of 1987, it would start up a fully-automated "factory of the future" capable of running 24 hours a day, seven days a week. GM said it would utilize knowledge acquired from a jointly operated GM-Toyota plant.

Matsudai's Kyoto dealership
MATSUDAI MOTORS
As you all know, Toyote Motors launched a big marketing offensive last fall. Everyone from number two Nissin on down is fighting back...
We've beefed up our sales force here—
But for us here at Matsudai, with the smallest market share of all, this is a matter of life or death!
The strong yen has ruined the export market and turned domestic sales into a bloody battleground!
yet our results haven't improved one damn bit!
So get out there and show a little fighting spirit— remember, every car you sell helps!!

What's he mean, results haven't improved?! You and I have been selling cars left and right!
Yeah, who's making us all look bad, anyway?!
Well, no matter how hard up they say they are, it's tough selling cars without any kind of marketing incentives!
Oh yeah— you know that no-good son of the bookstore owner on Motomachi Street? I hear he totalled his car in a collision with a truck last night...
Gotcha! I'll sell him a new 4WD* before he knows what hit him!
Oh no you don't, pal— he's mine!!
......
Hey, Suzuki...
But I'm such a klutz, and I know I'm dragging the curve down for everyone. I'm completely new to this market, I don't know local business practices...
Thanks, I appreciate that...
Don't listen to those idiots. You're giving it your best shot, and that's what counts!

* 4WD: Four-wheel drive vehicles, intended for off-road driving but now fashionable even in cities. Four-wheel drive improves performance in snow, mud, etc. One in ten new vehicles is now a 4WD.

Times have changed — nowadays 80% of auto sales are trade-ins. So the whole trick is to grab onto a first-time customer and never let go.
That makes it hard as hell to cultivate new customers from scratch...
Well, as you know, there are lots of guys like me
who suddenly got pushed into sales when the Hiroshima plant had to slash production because of the high yen. And now the company's seriously thinking about building cars in the U.S.
Not only that, they're making us sell cheap imports from their Taiwan subsidiary...
I understand the logic behind these moves, but it still feels to me like the company's shooting itself in the foot.
I just don't know what to think...
Huh! I can't really see bottom-ranked Matsudai trying to set itself up in America...
But if we lose this war,
what's going to happen to Matsudai? We've got 15,000 employees—that's 50,000 people counting our families. How're we gonna eat?
Yeah... I guess we have to win this one or die trying!

RRUMBLE
Oh, by the way my son is friends with the son of the fella who runs the pottery shop across from Kiyosumi Temple.
Apparently he's getting married soon, so I bet he'll be wanting to buy a new car...
Wow! Thanks for the tip!

REIMPORTS: Mazda announced plans to import cars it had built in the U.S. back to Japan starting in the summer of 1988, the first such move by a Japanese automaker and a vivid demonstration that the high yen has eliminated Japanese industry's cost advantage over the U.S.

I'll check it out right away!
My, my! So, were you able to make a sale?
Um, excuse me.
I'd like to buy this, please!
Will that be all, sir?
Er, actually ...
I understand you're getting married—congratulations!
Huh?
I heard from your friend Mr. Yamamoto...
and I was wondering, would you like to buy a car?!

I can guarantee you an excellent discount!!
I do need a car,
but I was already planning to buy one from another dealer...
Ulp! W-who would that be?!
We'll match their price, and better!
A Toyote Carrola
for 890,000 yen...
What?!
We couldn't possibly break even if we sold our cars for that little! The best I could do would be 950,000...
POTTERY CENTER
Well, the president of the dealership is the chairman of our local Merchants Association—he's a big cheese in these parts...
Even if you matched his price, I'd sorta have to buy from the Chairman, y'know what I mean?
Besides, they're selling Toyotes at real bargain prices these days!!
......

THE IMPORT TREND: Imports of foreign cars into Japan jumped 36.2% in 1986 thanks to prices reduced by the strong yen and lower loan interest rates; 68,300 imports were sold that year. West German cars were the overwhelming favorite, followed by British, Swedish, and American imports.

Thank you! Please come again!
>SOB<
FLASH

NIC AUTO INDUSTRIES: In 1985, South Korea produced some 380,000 cars. The Korean Big Three are Hyundai, Kia, and Daewoo. Taiwanese automakers, led by Yulong, produced 150,000 cars in 1985.

RRUMBLE
I was so depressed... I didn't even realize I'd walked all the way to Professor Funaoka's house.
So that's how I happened to run into you...
I see...
Sure! Sorry I wound up boring you
with my tales of woe...
Look, the rain's letting up!
Shall we go?
Hm?
Oh, that reminds me!
Not at all! In fact, your story is quite relevant to the work I'm doing!

I'd like to buy a car from you. After all, I'll need one while I'm here...
Wow! R-really?!
After three months—
BOO HOO HOO
I finally sold one!!
YAHOO!!

RANKING BY OUTPUT: Of the top twenty automakers worldwide, nine are Japanese, with Toyota ranked no. 1, Nissan no. 4, and Mazda no. 10.

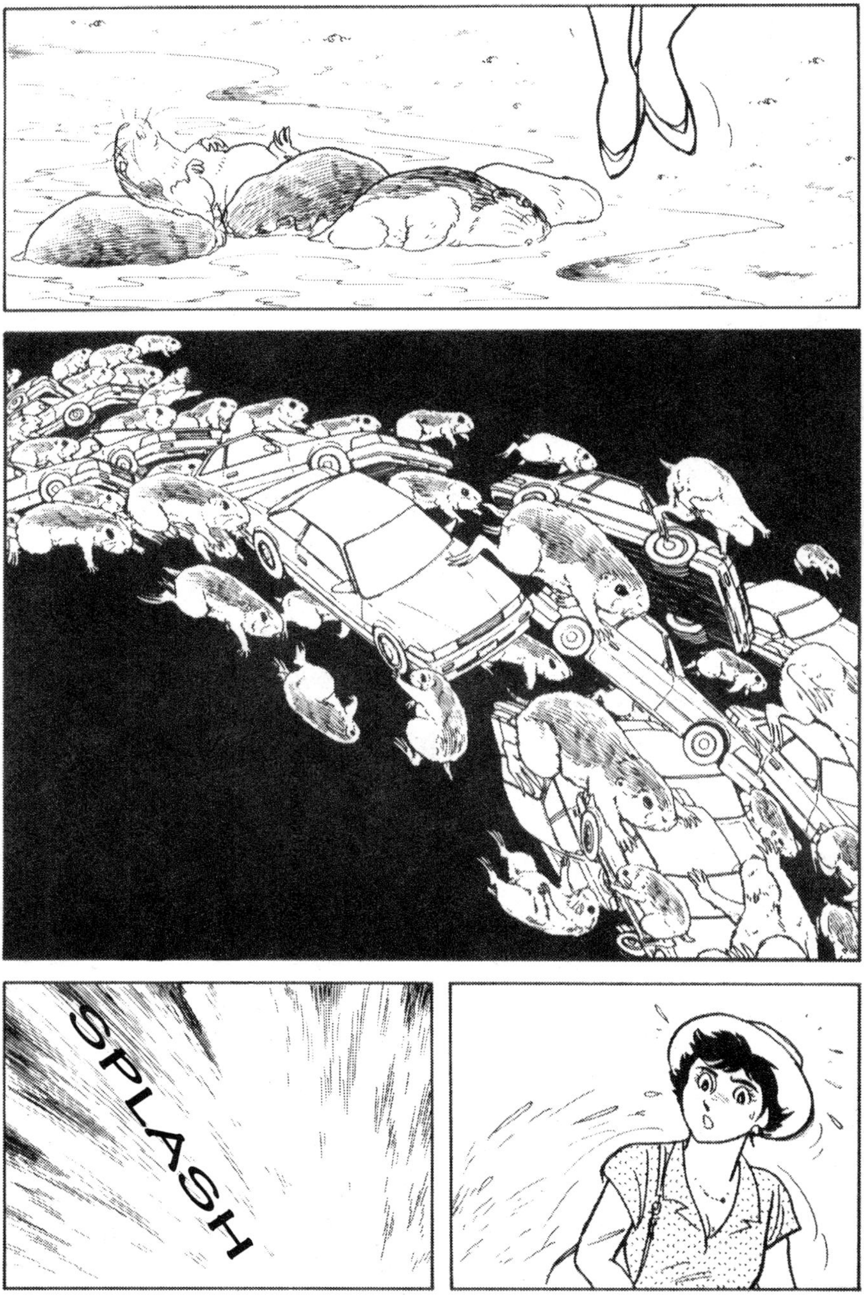
SPLASH

CHINESE MARKET: The Chinese auto market is expected to take off in the near future. Currently there is only one car per 300 Chinese citizens. Mitsubishi, Isuzu, and other Japanese automakers are already hatching production plans aimed at this market.

HOTEL PLATON

2-1, KIOI-CHO, CHIYODA-KU
TOKYO, JAPAN
PHONE : 03-379-5459

The importance of the auto industry to Japan can't be underestimated. Automakers, dealerships, and auto parts manufacturers and distributors together employ 5.12 million people -- 9.9% of all employees in Japan. If you include their families, over 12 million Japanese -- 10% of the population -- make their living from the automobile.

Japanese exports by product (1985)

Total: $175,640 million

Automobiles:	24%	($42,230 million)
Machinery:	16.8%	
Radios, TVs:	7.8%	
Steel:	7.7%	
Chemicals:	4.4%	
Scientific, optical:	3.9%	
Fibers:	3.6%	
Ships:	3.4%	
Metals, nonmetals:	2.8%	

"Car wars" are bound to escalate on a global scale. There's nothing anyone can do to prevent this, and no one should! Fierce competition in other industries -- coal, aluminum, steel, shipbuilding, word processors, calculators, watches -- has led to overproduction, lower prices, and the collapse of many a business. But this process is good for the consumer.

An economy can grow only through ruthless competition. For precisely that reason, government must provide a level playing field for competition and serve as referee. The "voluntary restraints" on exports ofJapanese cars to the U.S. ultimately put money in the pockets of the Big Three and the Japanese automakers at the expense of the American consumer. Likewise, protection of Japanese farming interests comes at the expense of urban office workers. Suppression of competition is not in the public interest -- quite the opposite! But when the battle is over, it is government's responsibility to play Florence Nightingale. It must come to the aid of wounded businesses and offer their employees a helping hand through job placement and retraining --just as Nightingale tended to the fallen in the Crimean War...

Estimated supply of automobiles in U.S. (for 1990)
(x 1000 vehicles)

1. Domestic production capacity		
GM:	6000	
Ford:	2100	
Chrysler:	1400	
AMC:	300	
Japanese makers:	1900	
Volkswagen:	200	
Hyundai:	100	
Total:	**12000**	(1)
Exports to Canada:	**1000**	(2)
Supply in U.S. (1)-(2):	**11000**	(3)
2. Imports		
Japanese:	2200	
German:	800	
Other:	750	
Total:	3750	(4)
3. Potential supply to U.S. (3)+(4):	**14750**	

From Nikkei Business, 12-8-86

③ Software Sting

"Knowledge is the only instrument of production that is not subject to diminishing returns." — J.M. Clark

The ABI Holmes Research Center near Albany, New York
With a 70% share of the global mainframe market, ABI (American Business Instruments) is the world's largest computer maker. The Holmes Lab Is ABI's "brain," its strategic R&D command...
Sawako is visiting the lab at the invitation of ABI's vice-president of technical development.

Right now, Sue here is working on a voice recognition* system for microcomputers.
If we can perfect that, you won't need to type everything out on a keyboard anymore.
You'll be able to issue verbal commands to the computer, and it'll interpret what you say and respond accordingly!
Incredible! Would I be able to do word processing by voice too?!
Typing's always been my nemesis, so let me know as soon as you have one ready —
I'll be your first customer!
Sure!
The machine will spell what you say correctly, and even check your grammar for errors!
This system's almost at the alpha test stage, so you should be able to try it out real soon!

* VOICE RECOGNITION: Technology by which a computer recognizes spoken words. The major hurdle is the conversion of sounds to characters. Currently a device the size of a suitcase is required to process 500 words.[This was written in the mid-Eighties—Ed.]

With systems like this on the market,
ABI's share is only going to keep growing!
Well, that brings me to one of the reasons we asked you up here, Miss Matsumoto.
We plan to build a lab similar to this one in Japan.
Is there something I can do to help?
There are signs that our market share is eroding over there. We want to reverse the trend by coming up with a long-term strategy for developing products geared to the Japanese market.
All our Japan business is handled by ABI Japan — but company policy calls for all R&D to be closely supervised by headquarters here in the States.
Well, I'd be happy to do anything I can — after all,
So we were hoping you could provide us with advice on such matters as location and hiring, Miss Matsumoto.
ABI has been one of Manhattan Trust's most valued clients for many years...

For ABI, Japan is both our biggest market and our toughest!
Since we never disclose data about our performance, I can't give you precise figures, but I can tell you this:
Are Japanese computer manufacturers really that formidable?!
Indeed they are!
The compatible* makers in particular...
there's a substantial gap between our share of the Japanese market and our global share!
By "compatible," you mean their computers can be used in place of ABI's without any special adjustments?
They're constantly undercutting us by building cheaper systems that can run the same software as ours! It drives us crazy!
Right!
They target our users, try to get 'em to switch to their systems
by promising them a machine with the same specs as ours, but 30% cheaper!
......

* COMPATIBLE: A computer built by one company that can run software programs written for another company's computer, without any alterations in the software.

And that strategy is paying off for them!
We've got to fight back somehow, or we'll have the devil to pay...
And that's why you want to focus on product development for the Japanese market — I see.
Exactly!
Japanese is a very distinct language. No matter how superb this new system here is, it won't sell too well in Japan if all it can process is English!
I see your point.
Well, I'd be happy to help out with any site research you need done!
Thank you! But that's not all...
Obviously, we've got to develop a truly Japanese-compatible product...
There will be other matters in which the company wishes to enlist your assistance, I believe.
Such as...?
>CHUCKLE<
Let's just say we've got some other cards up our sleeve as well!

"Other cards"?!
Certainly! This is well worth a look, Sawako!
......!?
But let's save that for another time.
Sue, could you show Miss Matsumoto our new supercomputer?*
Ichigaya, Tokyo: headquarters of Shikishima Tsushin Ltd. (Known as "Shikitsu")
Shikitsu is one of Japan's top computer makers. It has profited handsomely by manufacturing ABI-compatible systems, and is eating steadily into ABI's market share...

* SUPERCOMPUTER: A very fast computer capable of processing the voluminous data and complex formulas required in such fields as nuclear power, aerospace, and meteorology.

Goyo Bank's Hiroshi Okada is visiting Shikitsu's managing director. Goyo is Shikitsu's main bank.
My congratulations to you
on Shikitsu's stellar performance of late!
Why, thank you!
At this rate you'll be passing up ABI in mainframe sales in no time
and grabbing the top share of the Japanese market!
Well, ABI's never discounted its products anywhere in the world — yet I hear they're going to slash prices 20% in Japan.
Ah, but when your rival commands 70% of the global market
that's easier said than done !
I'd say that's proof positive of Shikitsu's strength!
...Once a user buys an ABI system, they have to keep upgrading it.
And every time they do, they have to pay through the nose for the privilege. Those customers aren't happy campers!

Well, we try to compensate for not being the leader in development by paying close attention to our users' needs...
Speaking of which, we're very grateful that Goyo Bank has decided to switch from ABI to Shikitsu for your third-generation online system!*
Heh heh! Shikitsu's compatibility is certainly a plus in that respect!
We can make the switch with no effort at all...
As the information revolution heats up,
everyone is being forced to upgrade to higher-capacity systems.
Our strategy is to pick up new customers when the time comes for them to replace their old machines.
I guess the proof's in the pudding!
The fact that Shikitsu is now poised to overtake the frontrunner
would suggest that your strategy is a resounding success!
That's kind of you, Mr. Okada —
but it's far too early to celebrate!

* THIRD-GENERATION ONLINE SYSTEM: An online network for Japan's city banks. Its second-generation predecessor streamlined interbank operations; the third generation links banks to homes and businesses.

Actually, that's the reason I asked you here today.
Oh...?
As you're probably aware, the U.S. revised its copyright law* last year.
ABI has been actively lobbying Congress over this issue for some time...
You're referring to the law that expanded copyrights
to include computer software, right?!
Right.
Under the revised law, ABI evidently intends to copyright all its programs
and keep the most crucial code secret!
Meaning that other companies wouldn't be able to copy ABI's programs, eh?
But I thought ABI's whole strategy was to conquer the world by making their own specs the global standard!
Well, it looks like they're in the process of switching to a new approach altogether.
They're running scared...!

* REVISION OF U.S. COPYRIGHT LAW: In 1980, Congress revised U.S. copyright law to expand legal protection to computer software. Japan followed suit in 1985.

They're continuing to lose Japanese market share to compatible makers like us and Joyo!
If the same thing happens to them in a third market, in Europe, say, it'll undermine their entire global strategy.
So they appear to be working out a plan of attack to stop us in our tracks!
...By preventing you from using their software at all?!
Well, they can't make the law apply retroactively, so we don't face any problem with what we're currently using.
But how will we acquire the source code for their next model?
That's the big question!
Has ABI made any kind of announcement?
Nope, not yet.
The law's still new, so it's not yet clear how it's going to be enforced in practice.

And consequently,
we don't yet know how to protect ourselves, either.
So how
can I help you in all this?
Ah yes, I was coming to that! We'd like to avail ourselves of your investigative talents and ask you to check out the Stateside situation for us!
ABI's intentions, Justice Department policy, developments in Congress — that sort of thing. We're doing our own investigations, of course, but our boys tend to come up with nothing but technical data!
I see... Well, our bank certainly ought to be concerned about this issue, since it could affect the entire information industry.
After all, the latest buzzword is the software-based economy, right? This has ramifications for all Japanese industries!
Please do what you can to help us out, Mr. Okada. With your American business school background,
this should be right up your alley!
I'll do my best!

HARDWARE: The physical components of a computer system, notably its central processing unit and main memory, which can function only as instructed by software programs.

New York: headquarters of Shikitsu America Inc.
ABI's notorious for its secretive ways, so I realize this will be no easy chore...
An employee of Joyo USA pays a visit to his counterpart at Shikitsu...
Any fresh news since the last time we talked?
Nah... We don't have a clue about ABI's plans!
They haven't leaked a thing about the programs that run their next big system, the 8008.
I'm getting pressure from my headquarters too.
Ordinarily we'd know all about their specs by now, but this time we're completely in the dark!

At this rate, there's gonna be a helluva time lag while we play catch-up after the 8008 hits the market.
Yeah, there's a real possibility ABI'll be able to recoup the share we fought so hard for...
Look, we may be rivals back in Japan, but here in the States we have a common enemy — so let's keep each other posted, okay?
You bet. If ABI really does deny us access to its code, we're both gonna be stuck between a rock and a hard place.
I think we've got to hang together on this one —
otherwise we'll hang separately, agreed?
Agreed!
By the way, this isn't 100% certain yet, but
we may be able to obtain the latest version of the entire code for the current 7007!
WHAT?!
Y-you're joking!!

But how? By what route?!
The new 7007 code hasn't even been released yet — if we get it now, we could save ourselves six months of development!
I know, it sounds almost too good to be true.
But if it *is* true, are you guys willing to work with us?
If we go halves on it, it'll be less painful to pay whatever it costs us!
You sure there's nothing underhanded about this?!
To get hold of unreleased code, somebody's gonna have to sneak it out of there somehow, aren't they?! Sounds pretty shady to me!
Hey, where it came from is none of our concern!
But you can bet if we don't come up with something soon, the top brass in Tokyo are gonna be really pissed off!
Yeah, yeah, I know...
But you can't be too careful when you're operating in a foreign country...
Of course.
Trust me, we'll move very carefully on this!

SOFTWARE: The programs and other documentation required to make a computer system work, including the system software that controls the computer and application software that performs various tasks.

The Tokyo office of Manhattan Trust
Hey-hey, Sawako!
Welcome back!
Hi, Bob.
How was New York?!
Same as ever!

It's no different than Tokyo — all hustle and bustle. Everyone's out buying up real estate...
At this rate, the entire surface of the planet
is gonna be Japanese-owned!
Mostly Japanese investors, from what I've heard!
Yeah, right!
But if we went back to the States, it'd be the same there — think about it!
No, really!
We're renting space here in a building owned by a Japanese landlord, right?
I suppose so... if America's trade and budget deficits keep growing like they are now...
Huh? What's the connection between real estate
and the deficits?
That's straight out of Economics 101!
Oh, come on, Bob!
Guess you haven't been reading your Nikkei Journal!

PROGRAMMING LANGUAGE: A system of symbols and rules for writing the instructions that run a computer in a form the computer can understand. Each new version of a language yields a new generation of software.

As long as the red ink flows, the dollar keeps falling and the yen keeps rising.
When the yen rises, American real estate gets cheaper, and Japanese investors snap more of it up!
Hoo boy! Sounds like one of those complicated Kabuki plots!
Oh, it's much more logical than that!
...Speaking of the trade deficit, I'd like to get some advice from you on a related subject.
What's that?
No wait, lemme guess! You've got a plan
to eliminate America's trade deficit with Japan!
Exactly!
Wow! Where do I fit into that?!
My current assignment is to help ABI recover the market share it's lost over here.
Well, first off,

I want you to give me a crash course in the computer business.
You know far more than I do about the industry in Japan!
O.K. O.K.
How about tonight—
while we partake of a little libation?!
Sounds good to me!
>GIGGLE<
Say no more!
President's Office
ABI headquarters, New York
Heh heh heh! Yep, they went right for it!
Just like a bunch of greedy little piranhas...
Well, the fish have grabbed the bait!
Now all we have to do is quietly reel 'em in till it's too late for them to get away...

NEUMANN COMPUTER: In 1946, the mathematician John von Neumann proposed the design of the present-day computer, which would store programs in an internal memory and perform serial processing of data.

If you can really put the screws to 'em over this,
>CHUCKLE<
it'll be a big load off our minds, I can tell you!!
Look, we only took action to demonstrate that we don't take crimes of this sort lightly!
I must remind you that we're not doing this for the sake of one company's profits, or some kind of private vendetta!
This is part of an ongoing criminal investigation, no more, no less...
Of course, of course!
So... when do you plan to reel in these particular fish?!
Well, the plan is for the angler to contact 'em tomorrow evening! By the way,
will you be using the actual software as bait?
No way!
>SNORT<
It'll be a clever fake in which we've rewritten the most critical code!
An artificial lure, eh?!
>HMPH<
So those poor suckers are gonna get hooked snapping at flies they can't even eat!

Well, that's what they get for trying to make a quick buck by stealing someone else's product!
I'll let you know tomorrow night how our fishing expedition went.
Heh heh heh! I can hardly wait!
Akasaka: the Hotel Platon
Okay, let me get this straight.
Shikitsu and Joyo are compatible makers, which means their machines run the same programs as ABI's.
And then there's Yamato Electric and Mitsutomo,
which make non-compatible machines that use their own programs — but they're all fighting for a piece of ABI's pie!

NON-NEUMANN COMPUTER: A computer that performs concurrent, parallel processing of multiple instructions, unlike the serial-processing Neumann type. Parallel processing is one focus of Japan's Fifth Generation computer project.

You got it! Until the seventies, ABI was the only game in town —
but then companies like Shikitsu started building systems that could take the place of ABI's...
And now that even the non-compatibles are making inroads, ABI's starting to feel the squeeze. If you look at hardware alone, many say the Japanese machines are better than ABI's.
But whether or not that's true,
SWIZZLE SWIZZLE
no one can deny they're a lot cheaper!
Another big factor is the growing use of personal computers, right?
Right. It's becoming more and more common to hook a mainframe
up to a bunch of PCs that can be used concurrently in different locations. That's why the market share of PC makers like Yamato is growing.
ABI's still the undisputed leader, right?
Well, to some degree.
SLURP
But in terms of software programs, at least,
Okay,I can see now why the big daddy of the computer world is worried about the Japanese market.

It's true that the compatible makers have no choice but to copy ABI's programs to run their machines.
But since the software comes free when you purchase an ABI system, all they have to do is become ABI clients to get it!
Then all they've gotta do is write compatible programs...
So even ABI's software dominance is hardly a sure thing. It all boils down to price —
that's the main issue where compatibles are concerned!
But America recently revised its copyright law.
Now computer programs are protected as intellectual property too, aren't they?!
They haven't made any moves in that direction yet.
But ABI did some heavy-duty lobbying to get that copyright revision passed —
which would suggest that sooner or later, they'll make a move!
Don't you think ABI will use that as a weapon to prevent the copying of their code?
And if they do...

COMPUTER GENERATIONS: The development of the computer is described in terms of its circuitry. The first generation of computers used vacuum tubes, the second, transistors, the third, integrated circuits (ICs), and the fourth, very large scale integrated circuits (VLSIs).

What will the compatible makers do then?!
Well, they can write their own programs —
or they can try to license the code from ABI!
But if they have to write the code from scratch, what's the point of being compatible?!
What indeed! And if they try to work out a deal with ABI,
you can bet ABI will make them pay dearly for the privilege — and there goes their price advantage!
In a nutshell, they're screwed either way!
...I see.
So computers are a key technology in America's efforts to hang onto its position of dominance!
I expect ABI will launch its counterattack when conditions are right.
That's why they called on you, Sawako— to help lay the groundwork!
You know, I can't help thinking the U.S. government is working behind the scenes on this...
Hmm
I haven't heard anything for sure about that.

But I do know that the U.S. has been pushing Japan to pass software protection legislation of its own.
So it's a pretty safe bet there's some serious power politicking going on!
......
The Planning Office of Goyo Bank
GOYO BANK
Okada!!
Something terrible's happened!!
?!
I just got a call from the Foreign Ministry.
Employees of Shikitsu and Joyo have been arrested in the U.S. by the FBI!!
WHAT?!
Th-the hell you say!!

FIFTH GENERATION COMPUTERS: The next generation of computers is expected to be a quantum leap beyond the current generation in technology as well as theory; the Fifth Generation project aspires to develop a computer that more closely resembles the human brain.

I don't have the details yet,
but they were busted trying to buy stolen computer software!!
Was it ABI's?!
Yep!
Two guys, one from Shikitsu and one from Joyo, went to pick it up...
and the FBI was waiting for 'em and nabbed 'em on the spot!!
A setup, eh?!
Must've been a sting operation —
Bastards!
staged by the U.S. government in cahoots with ABI!
We better start thinking about damage control...
This is gonna be big trouble, Okada...
If Shikitsu really did screw up bigtime,
Goyo may get caught in the backwash, too!
PUFF PUFF
PACE PACE
The whole thing's outrageous!!

Shikitsu headquarters
The FBI nabbed one of your boys and one of ours...
Apparently they were lured into buying the new software for the 7007...
No, that's all I know. That's what our Stateside attorney told me when he called.
...Well, I'll be taking the next flight to New York.
How about you?
...Uh-huh. Yeah, we've got to move very carefully, or the shit could really hit the fan...

OPERATING SYSTEM: The basic system software that runs a computer. Positioned between other programs and the hardware itself, the operating system controls input/output, storage and other basic operations.

Manhattan Trust's Tokyo office
A sting operation, eh?!
The FBI really got down and dirty on this one!
'Course, that's their usual modus operandi when they're determined to nail somebody... If nothing else, this makes the U.S. government's intentions perfectly clear!
That's entrapment, isn't it?!
To deliberately entice someone into committing a crime...
Yeah, yeah, I know...
This sort of operation wouldn't be legal over here.
But don't you think that's pretty sleazy?!
But the American view of the law is different from Japan's.
Even if you're lured into committing a crime, you're still guilty of it!
In a lot of cases, though, you can cut a deal in court and stay out of jail...
......

Well, in this case, I doubt they care if the suspects get off or not.
The real point is that Shikitsu and Joyo walked right onto a land mine laid for them by ABI!
Yep... We should look at it as ABI's opening gambit in their counteroffensive against Japan!
But this is just a preview.
We ain't seen nothin' yet!
Sawako...
What about you? You put on your yukata
Oh, gimme a break, Bob!
As a Japanese, you may end up wishing you hadn't taken this job!
and traipse on down to the public baths like a good Japanese —
but deep down, you're still a Yankee!
Ha ha! Sure, I'm an American citizen,
but my granddaddy emigrated there from Ireland!

APPLICATION PROGRAMS: The application software, written in a programming language, that performs actual tasks on a computer, such as engineering calculations, inventory management, business analysis, and so on.

Me, I make my home wherever I live!
Several months have elapsed since the industrial spy sting. ABI has filed suit, and the case is pending in court. The publicity generated in the U.S. media has hurt Shikitsu badly.
Shikitsu headquarters
Mr. Okada!

This fiasco has been a disaster for us!
But the worst of it is, we should have seen a scam like that a mile away!
......
It's our own damn fault for being so hasty...
...The U.S. government conspired with a private corporation
to entrap a Japanese business, that's all!
Their real objective was to give the American public the impression that Japan plays dirty pool!
After seeing trade friction erupt in one sector after another — fibers, steel, autos, semiconductors — they decided early on that the next showdown would be over computers!
Shikitsu just happened to get caught in the crossfire!
I suppose you're right...

ONLINE REAL-TIME PROCESSING: The input and processing of data as soon as it is generated, made possible by hooking up a computer to communication lines and installing input/output terminals at each data generating site.

Still, ABI has plotted its moves very cleverly this time.
They're not going to settle for chicken feed.
Negotiations on a settlement aren't going well for us...
Didn't they also serve notice that they wouldn't provide their source code anymore?
Yes, they made the announcement right in the midst of the settlement talks.
Looks like they'll be completely dropping their old policy, starting with the software for their new 8008 model.
Then, while we're still groggy,
they follow up with a body blow — no more code!
In fact, the sting appears to have been a sort of sucker punch to soften us up!
If you lose access to their code,
will it be impossible for you to write compatible programs?
It would be hell to assemble 'em by trial and error, based on minimal information...
You might wind up with a program in which several critical functions were unusable, for example...
Hmm...

Sounds like that would make it damn hard to replace ABI systems with your own...
Up to now, almost as soon as ABI hit the market with a new product, we'd be right behind 'em with our own version.
But if we have to slap a program together ourselves, even supposing we can produce one that works, it'll take far too long...
It would.
Our whole compatibility strategy would go down the tubes!
In the time it would take us, ABI could develop a brand new product.
So what are your plans for dealing with the situation?!
Well, the most palatable option seems to be
to sign a deal with ABI permitting us to use their software—
in other words, pay a royalty to license the code.
The trouble with that is, we have no idea
how much information ABI's willing to part with!

PERSONAL COMPUTER: A general-purpose microcomputer for use by an individual. PCs are easier to write programs for than mainframe computers, and are well suited to nonstandard tasks.

Judging by recent developments, there's no way they're going to provide us with all the code we need!
But
you can't produce programs like that overnight, can you?!
So our only alternative may be to change course completely, and develop programs on our own that are as good as or better than ABI's!
Unfortunately, no.
We'll just have to keep ponying up royalties
while we try to develop better software as fast as we can,
and market it to other users, not just ABI's...
The question, then, is how much of its hand is ABI going to show from now on, right?
Right...
Apropos of which,
I have a very big favor to ask of you, Mr. Okada...
Yes?

Our company will require a large infusion of funds in the immediate future — both for the settlement with ABI, and for the code-licensing royalties we'll have to pay for some time to come...
We'd like your bank to help us out.
I'll speak to our Credit Department about it right away.
Thank you very much. One more thing —
I-is there something else?!
If we *are* able to reach an agreement with ABI, it will no doubt be under conditions of complete secrecy.
Up to now, it's been their policy not to divulge one iota of information about agreements of this sort.
ABI's known for refusing to make anything public — not just sales and profit figures, but even the size of their payroll!
That's true.
It's rare for so little to be known about a company so big...
The problem, Mr. Okada, is that to ABI,
"secret" means we can't even tell our main bank!

PATTERN RECOGNITION: The ability to recognize and process graphics, three-dimensional images, sounds and the like — a much more complex process than recognizing characters and symbols. Development of a pattern recognition system that comes close to mimicking human sense perception faces many hurdles.

What?!
Y-you mean, you expect us to help you finance an agreement without even knowing what it contains?!
I'm terribly sorry, but that's the only way we'd be allowed to do it.
Just this once, I ask you — in light of our long-standing relationship — please help us out, no questions asked!!
I-I'll see what I can do...
Washington: U.S. Department of Commerce
DEPARTMENT OF COMMERCE

Commerce Secretary Baldwin meets with ABI Chairman Akins...
So is everything going as planned?
Yep, can't complain, so far.
I must say, it hardly seems like an even match at this point, considering the Japanese computer makers have only a 5% share of the global market to your 70%...
No, I suppose not. Look what they did to our TV, auto and semiconductor industries! While we sit back and put 'em down as a bunch of imitators, their products are taking over the world...
Well, we can't afford to let our guard down!
Exactly! That's why we've got to be sure we nip 'em in the bud this time.
Otherwise, history will judge us as fools who deserved what we got!
Of course, computers are just part of the big picture.
The entire high-tech field is closely linked to our national security, so the President naturally takes a great interest in this issue...
>CHUCKLE<
Well, we've got a couple more cards up our sleeve yet -
so please tell the President we won't disappoint him!

INTERFACE: A component (or more loosely, any procedure or set of conditions) that links two computers or systems (such as a central processing unit and a peripheral device) that operate according to different specifications.

Sounds good!
I look forward to seeing what you come up with next!
Goyo Bank headquarters
Since they signed that code-licensing deal with ABI, Shikitsu's bottom line has taken a nose dive!!
That's because they've made some huge outlays right on the heels of that lump sum they paid to settle the spy case.
But that's not all.
Rumor has it ABI forced 'em to agree to pay 100 billion yen a year in royalties!

Well, since Shikitsu won't tell us a damn thing, we don't know if that's true or not.
But if it is, Shikitsu will go into the red as early as next year.
That bad, eh?!
Goyo has done all it can to help Shikitsu grow — after all, it's the flagbearer of our domestic computer industry...
TAP TAP
But now...?! Any truth to that rumor, Okada?
My guess is it's one figure lower.
But even so, if you add an expenditure that size to the adverse effect of the strong yen, you'll see a plunge in their profits, no doubt about it!
Well, 100 billion a year
has got to be an exaggeration...
The big question is how soon they'll be able to ship their own programs and start showing improved results...
How many years d'you think that'll take?
I'd say three, if they push it.
Three years, eh...

BIT: A single binary digit, the smallest unit of information handled by a computer. One bit may represent two states, 0 or 1; two bits may represent four states, 00, 01, 10, or 11.

If we adhere to our normal lending standards,
we'll have a big decision to make sometime next year...
Surely we wouldn't send Shikitsu down the river?! MITI wouldn't stand for it, for one thing...
But we can't afford to be left holding the bag.
Even now, Shikitsu's stock continues to lose ground while the rest of the market is soaring...
ABI Japan headquarters
ABI
When I heard Manhattan Trust was sending over a senior economist, I had no idea it would be a lovely young lady like yourself!
What a pleasant surprise! American banks certainly are different from the ones we have here...
Really?

But your own company, ABI, prides itself on nurturing talented personnel
without regard for gender or age...
I met many young people in key positions at your U.S. headquarters!
Ha ha ha!
...I'm just glad that more and more companies are utilizing the talents of bright young women these days!
Admittedly, it's taking a while for Japanese businesses to catch on.
If I'm not mistaken, *you* became president of ABI Japan before you turned forty, didn't you?
But when I see women like you playing an active role in the global economy,
it makes me very optimistic about the future, Miss Matsumoto!
Oh my — I hardly deserve such praise!
I'm really not much more than a bank clerk at this point!
Well, let's get down to business. I understand you have some recommendations
about where to locate our new research center...

FLOPPY DISK: A form of external storage media used with a computer, consisting of a flexible polyester disk coated with magnetic material and sheathed in a square jacket.

I've been told by U.S. headquarters to pay heed to your opinion on this matter!
Here's a report I've prepared for you. I'll be glad to go over it later
with the people in charge of the project.
But there's something else I wanted to ask you about — strictly out of personal curiosity. May I...?
Go right ahead! I'll answer as best I can — you represent our bank, after all!
Lately your company seems to be doling out some pretty strong medicine to the Japanese compatible makers...
I'm wondering, does ABI intend to drive them out of business?
My oh my! That's quite a question!
>CHUCKLE<
Well, the Japanese media is blowing a lot of hot air about it —
but that's really not our intention.
We're hardly powerful enough to seal their fate all by ourselves!
......

As for the software copyright issue, that's ABI's lifeblood. Naturally we're going to assert our proprietary rights in that area...
Up to now, after all, we've seen our property copied in what you could hardly call a fair and square manner!
But hasn't ABI deliberately encouraged that, as a way of making your software the global standard?!
That may be how it looks from the outside, but it's always been our intention to protect our property.
However, our top priority has been the convenience of the user, so we couldn't just declare everything off limits...
Then why have you decided to declare your software off limits now?!
For purely technical reasons!
With the tremendous advances we've achieved in data processing technology, our programs have become extremely complex.If we continue to provide them to our users, they'll be tempted to fiddle with 'em, which could cause problems with the machines they're supposed to run.
Even so,

HACKER: A trespasser on a computer system. Since the early eighties, hackers have posed a problem for U.S. military and university computer systems, which they illegally access, sometimes rewriting or destroying data.

I gather this has come as a serious blow to Shikitsu and Joyo...
Heck, they've been writing stuff *we'd* love to copy for some time now! It's just a matter of time before they come storming back with software better than ours...
Oh no, far from it!
Sure, it may be rough going for a while, but they're eminently capable of developing their own programs!!
But there are those who say ABI's recent actions reflect its desire for world domination!
Oh, come now!
That's a rather xenophobic reaction, don't you think?
After all, I'm the president of ABI Japan, and I'm Japanese! So are most of our employees!
Whoever makes the user happiest, wins!
We're just talking about business as usual here, aren't we?!
......

A Shikitsu sales office
...I'm terribly sorry.
Yes, I know the shipping date is coming up soon. Unfortunately, the program isn't ready yet...
Yes, I'll relay your concerns to our program development department...
BOW SCRAPE GROVEL
I'm very, very sorry.
No, no... it won't be that long a delay...
I'm afraid I can't...
Not another complaint about the program delay?!
I'm getting sick of this!
What the hell is headquarters up to?!
I hear they've got everyone working on their mainframe microcode, so all the special-order customer programs have been put on the back burner...
Fallout from ABI's new policy, eh...
If this keeps up, all our customers are gonna jump ship!
If we don't do something soon, we won't have anyone left to sell to!
......
BOW SCRAPE

PASSWORD: A code identifying someone who has permission to use the information stored on a computer. For security purposes, users must enter this code before they can use the computer.

Sawako, didja hear the news?
No, what?
Manhattan Trust's Tokyo office
ABI's filed a claim with the arbitration association accusing Shikitsu of violating their code-licensing agreement!
Yeah, they're saying a section of that new program Shikitsu went to all that trouble to develop infringes on ABI's copyright!
Apparently the agreement didn't cover that part...
WHAT?!
You're joking!
Wow, the hits just keep coming, don't they!
It seems like ABI doesn't want to quit...
If ABI has its way, Shikitsu will have to fork over mucho damages again, this time for breach of contract!!

Insult to injury, eh...
How do Shikitsu's chances look?
I asked our legal advisor about it.
He says recent precedents in American courts give ABI the edge!
I see...
So now they've got the Justice Department on their side along with Commerce...
With an All-American lineup like that, Shikitsu doesn't stand much of a chance!
"All-American lineup"...?!
Goyo Bank's Planning Office
They're saying Shikitsu's gonna have to pay ABI 300 billion yen if they lose this case!
Hey, Okada!
Our credit department's having a collective coronary... Is that figure right?!
...They're in trouble, that's for sure!
That secret deal they signed is a piece of work.
ABI took advantage of the fact that Japanese lawyers are still green in the computer business.

JAPANESE INFORMATION PROCESSING: The ability to process and store Japanese characters (kanji and kana) on a computer; an obvious prerequisite for the marketing of computer systems in Japan.

Shikitsu argues they developed the code entirely on their own —
and that much is true.
But ABI is claiming that the "logical foundation" of the code is the same as theirs!
WHA—?!
How can a trumped-up charge like that stand?!
You're saying Shikitsu didn't catch it on their own?!
Guess they walked right into another high-tech trap!!
Evidently that's the real reason ABI insisted on keeping the agreement secret.
If it were made public, someone would've noticed something fishy in the fine print...
They rushed into that agreement while they were still reeling from the spy case.
Obviously, they didn't pay close enough attention.
Even so, that's really overkill on ABI's part!
Now they'll go into the red for sure!!
Shikitsu's share would still be dropping without this extra shove!
......

A major customer of Shikitsu
Two of the most important functions of the ABI program are missing from Shikitsu's version.
I know, and we've got to have those functions for our business!
I guess we have no choice but to go with ABI...
That's gonna cost us at least 30% more!
ABI's feeling its oats these days — they won't discount a thing!
Yeah, and I hear ABI's manufacturing cost for their computers is less than 30%!
Those sleazebags! Is that any way to run a business?!
I just wish our domestic makers would get off their butts!
Their hardware is already second to none, for God's sake!
You are correct, sir!!

MACHINE TRANSLATION: The automatic translation of text from one language to another (e.g. Japanese to English) by computer. Current machine translation systems use three steps: syntactic analysis of the source text, conversion, and generation of the target text.

Sawako!
Why, Hiroshi!
Where you headed?
Kyoto, to pay a visit to Professor Funaoka!
Uh, Sawako...?
Yes?
Never mind.
See you later!

Kyoto: the residence of Soichiro Funaoka

BAR CODE: A code expressed by the number, length, and width of a series of bars and dots. Bar codes are used as product codes for point-of-sale systems in supermarkets and other retail outlets.

Been a while, hasn't it!
What're you up to these days?
I'm helping ABI with their Japanese operations...
Ho ho!
So you're one of the masterminds behind that Shikitsu affair, are you?
Oh, please, Professor!
They'd never entrust me with high-stakes operations like that!
I'm just doing some research for them.
I came down here to check out a site ABI's picked for their new lab near Lake Biwa —
so I thought, since I'm in the area...
Ha ha ha!
You'd pay a visit to your old boyfriend, eh?
Actually,
I've been having second thoughts since that whole scandal broke...
Lemme guess!
You're feeling guilty about working for the Yanks, aren't you!

Don't be silly, my dear! If our side had their wits about 'em, they would've known what the Yanks were up to.
It's the fault of the Japanese companies and our government for ignoring the warning signs!
You think so...?
Sure! The U.S. government's been pushing like crazy to get Japan to pass its own software copyright law!
This last caper just happened to be the first overt action they took!
America decided the next big battleground would be high-tech, and they positioned themselves accordingly.
I guess you're right. I have a friend who believes this was a scenario cooked up by the White House...
No doubt!
And this is just the opening salvo.
We'll see more and more cases like it —
after all, the high-tech sector is cheek by jowl with the military!
Then what do you think Japan should do, Professor?

OA/HA: Office automation (OA) is the automation of business operations using computers and communications equipment; the corresponding technology for private households is called home automation (HA).

Good question!
I don't think we have any choice but to develop our own technology.
But our track record on domestic development is pretty pathetic —
and that's what led to the present brouhaha.
Japan is number one at improving and marketing technologies invented by someone else!
The compatible makers are like those little shark-sucking remoras...
They cling to the belly of the big shark, ABI, and steal its food...
But try as it might, a remora will never grow as big as the host shark...
Still, developing their own technology
is much easier said than done, Professor!

Of course! If it were so simple, it wouldn't count for anything!
But with the right application of money and human resources, there's no reason Japan can't become a world leader in the field!
Anyway, until our boys produce something that blows ABI out of the water,
you can bet the Yanks'll continue to give 'em hell!
And furthermore, my fellow Americans,
we must do everything we can
Look!
to preserve America's technological edge
if we are to regain our position of world leadership, both militarily and economically!

CAD/CAM: Computer aided design (CAD) and computer aided manufacturing (CAM) are technologies that utilize computers to design and manufacture products.

Our technology must be second to none, and we must spare no effort to achieve that goal! Even if our opponent is one of our closest allies, this is a contest we can't afford to lose!!

NEWS
...Elsewhere in his State of the Union address, President Reagan said...

Feels like winter's coming early this year, Sawako...

OPTICAL COMMUNICATION: The use of optical fiber (glass filament about 0.1 mm in diameter) instead of copper wire to transmit information over long distances via light instead of electricity. Optical fibers can transmit far more data than copper wire.

HOTEL PLATON

2-1, KIOI-CHO, CHIYODA-KU
TOKYO, JAPAN
PHONE : 03-379-5459

Back in 1982, the U.S. Cabinet Council on Commerce and Trade released a report titled *Evaluating the Competitiveness of American High-Technology Industries*. This document argu that: (A) High-tech industries were critical to the survival of the U.S. (B) These industrie were inextricably linked to national security. (C) Foreign governments had implemented closed-market policies to nurture this field to their advantage, and this was adversely affecting American high-tech industries. (D) America's biggest challenge in the field was Japan. (E) The Japanese challenge would grow more severe in the future. In other words, the race with Japan for dominance in the high-tech sector was only going to get tougher. The focus of U.S.-Japanese trade friction has shifted over the years in the direction of increasingly sophisticated technologies: from fibers to steel to color TVs to cars. Today semiconductors and computers are the big battleground. With their national security ramifications, these industries have become a political concern as well. When a Japanese computer manufacturer recently tried to buy out an American semiconductor maker, the U.S. government intervened to quash the deal— ample proof of the extent of America's anxiety over this issue. Trade friction between the two countries is bound to heat up as time goes by.

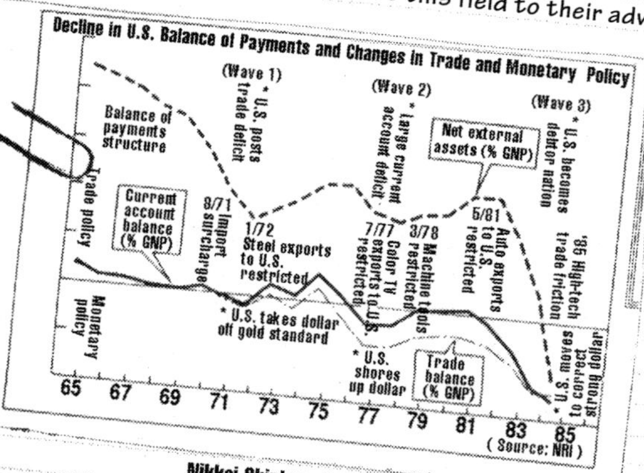

Nikkei Shinbun, 2-15-87

Table 7-8: Trends in Japanese Electronics Exports/Imports to/from U.S. (Unit: 100 million Yen)

Year	Industrial electronics		Electronic components		Semiconductors		Consumer electronics	
	Exports	Imports	Exports	Imports	Exports	Imports	Exports	Imports
1978	1008	1159	2093	828	174	407	5479	49
79	1211	1548	2707	1324	418	741	4429	77
80	1676	2047	3438	1406	724	696	4940	81
81	2905	2053	4130	1549	712	725	7734	71
82	4887	2394	4485	1886	1168	835	7162	54
83	7975	2340	6662	2165	1843	1076	9295	39
84	13058	2894	12253	3818	3722	1636	15399	44

(Source: MITI)

④ *The Great Wave*

“In estimating the prospects of investment, we must have regard... to the nerves and hysteria and even the digesting and reactions to the weather of those upon whose spontaneous activity it largely depends.”
— J.M. Keynes, *The General Theory of Employment, Interest, and Money*

JAPAN AIR LINES

Venice, Italy
June, 1987: the 13th Summit Conference*

* SUMMIT (1): The 13th summit of world leaders was held in 1987. The first such conference took place in 1975 in Rambouillet at the invitation of French President Giscard D'Estaing, followed by summits in the U.S., U.K., West Germany, Japan, Italy, and Canada.

I'm not gonna let you beat me this time, Yasu!

I'll show ya how we do it in the Wild West!!
Ha ha ha! You better watch it —
I've been honing my jujitsu skills tussling with the young upstarts in my own party!
See ya later, Yasu...
But I think we have the situation under control now.
I just hope you'll go easier on me than they have, Maggie!
You're having a hard time with those rioting students, aren't you, Francois!
Mais oui!
This is my ninth summit, you know.
I must say, they're getting a bit tedious!
I'm tired of this damned game we've been playing ever since Yasu came on board!
Well, it's a nice harmless way for us to get to know each other better, n'est-ce pas?
Au revoir, my dear!

SUMMIT (2): The 1987 summit, held in Venice, was ostensibly for working out details of the economic policies agreed upon at the Tokyo summit the previous year. However, critics charged that these summits were becoming no more than a political dog-and-pony show.

CLACK
CLACK
Lon!
I said "Lon," not "Ron" — that means I'm out!
You called, Yasu?
Sacre bleu! What's the damage?!

Well, I've only got Pin Fuu...
So that'll be $100 million.
>SNIFF< That's Japan for you—plodding along, saving up little by little...
Why don't you loosen up a bit, Yasu? You Japanese never seem to know how to separate work from play.
You could learn a little about joie de vivre from us Frenchmen!
I'm all out of dollars, myself!
That was my last $100 mil, and it all went to Yasu!
Yasu wins all the time! He's got too big a surplus!
At this rate, we won't be able to keep the game going!
Hey, I'm not doing anything wrong...
CLATTER
CLATTER CLATTER
Well, I expected something like this to happen —

so I brought along this handy dollar bill printing machine.
Print me $100 million, will ya?
Yessir!
Oh, that's lovely, Ron!
Now we can continue with our game!
Hmph! If you make it too easy to print money, it loses its value, don't you think?!
Well, what else can we do? Dollars are the only world currency we've got...
Yep, and I'm the guy whose job it is to supply the world with it!
...Lon!
I got another hit!
Lon, Lon, Lon — all you ever do is take my money!

SUMMIT (3): Of the heads of state who attended the Venice meeting, U.K. Prime Minister Thatcher had the longest attendance record; it was her ninth summit. It was the fifth for Nakasone, and the seventh for Reagan and Mitterrand.

You don't seem interested in trying to improve your gaming skills, Ron!
CLACK
We Europeans keep our guard up — that's why you don't see us losing so much!
Maggie's right, Ron! You don't have enough self-discipline!
For starters, stop relying on that damn printing machine — all it does is reduce the value of your dollars!
I agree —
so tell Yasu to stop winning so much!
Winners have to take some responsibility, but so do the losers!
As long as he's got his bloody printing machine,
GRAB
Ron refuses to listen to reason!
— Take that!!
SMASH

Good for you, Maggie!
It's Sayonara time for the dollar!
But we can't really drop the dollar just like that.
If we do, it'll plunge and we'll have a panic on our hands. All these dollars I've hoarded will be so much scrap paper!
From now on, let's use gold to cover our bets.
That way we'll all be forced to live within our means!
Thanks for that, Yasu!
Merde!!
You're a good buddy, you are!
This game is a lost cause!!
We never should've given those damn Yanks the Statue of Liberty.
This isn't freedom, it's a free-for-all!
I rue the day we let the Colonies win their little revolution!
Gentlemen must know their limits!!

SUMMIT (4): Lately it has become fashionable for the wives of summit leaders to participate as well. At the1986 Tokyo summit, the first ladies of West Germany, Italy, and Canada attended a Kabuki performance together, giving rise to the term "first ladies' diplomacy."

Here's the draft of the speech you'll be giving at the Venice summit tomorrow, Mister President!
GASP!
...Anyway, that was a funny story I read recently.
Ha ha ha!
That *is* funny!

I hear you're flying to New York again, Sawako.
Will you be gone for long this time?
I'm afraid so. Chairman Miller seems to have a lot on his mind...
I see.
Well, I'm going to miss you.
......
Homma-san...
JAPAN AIR LINES

IMF: The International Monetary Fund, which began operation in 1947, now claims as members nearly all Western nations and some from the former Communist bloc. With the World Bank, it takes the lead in providing financing for debtor nations to maintain global monetary stability.

Manhattan Trust headquarters, New York City
Sawako!
You brought the Bank Americana financial statement with you, didn't you?
Bank Americana — once the number-two bank in the U.S.!
What?
Did you say "once"?!
SNICKER

I thought Bank Americana was perfectly sound! Has something happened...?!
Heh heh heh!
Tell me, Sawako, where do most of Bank Americana's loans go?
Let's see—the biggest category is agricultural interests,* followed by energy-related industries...
They also make a lot of loans to third world countries...
— Every one of 'em a category that's not in the greatest shape, wouldn't you agree?!
Hmph!
Not only that, but unlike us, Bank Am hasn't gotten into electronic banking —
so now, with interest rates coming down, they're having a devil of a time staying competitive!
But still —
the Reagan Administration is doling out farm subsidies, and has kept oil prices propped up, hasn't it?
They'll be cutting the farm subsidies now that the budget deficit's gotten too big!
HAH!
And the energy slump is only gonna get worse!

* AGRICULTURAL RECESSION: The farming slump of the eighties affected the financial sector. In the U.S., commercial bank profits fell in 1986 for the first time in 25 years. In the same year, 68 agricultural banks failed.

Meanwhile, primary industry products will continue their decline for eight more years, so the debtor nations* will sink even deeper into debt!
H-how can you be so certain about these figures you're quoting?!
"For eight more years"?!
Ah, well, never mind that...
The point is, Bank Am's performance will continue to worsen, and its stock will nosedive!
We're gonna wait till the time is ripe, then launch our takeover bid** —
so what I want you to do is figure out what price we should make our offer at!
Takeover?!

* DEBTOR NATIONS: Brazil, Mexico and other developing countries bear huge burdens of external debt, and must continue to borrow to pay them off. Sluggish markets for farm products and oil have contributed to the cash flow crisis these nations face.

** TAKEOVER BID (TOB): The announcement of a price at which a party intends to purchase stock in a company from its shareholders in order to acquire a controlling interest in the company. A TOB can be cancelled if the bidder fails to acquire the targeted number of shares.

Our bank doesn't have even half the assets of Bank Americana!
It would be like an alligator trying to swallow an elephant! I think this plan makes no sense at all!!
Who asked you?!
I just want you to keep an eye on Bank Am, got that?!
You can go now!
BAM!
SUNSPOT DATA
SUNSPOT DATA

......
ZAP
SUNSPOT DATA
...Sunspot Data
"Sunspot Data"...?
I didn't realize the Chairman was interested in astronomy...
Anyway, this talk about taking over Bank Am is crazy!
A long time ago, Chairman Miller was fired by Costello, the Chairman of Bank Am...
I wonder if that's what this is all about?!
I don't want to believe he'd let a personal grudge skew his judgement.
But otherwise I can't make head or tail of what he's doing...

Hmm... Chairman
Miller was right —
Bank Am's performance is
a lot worse than I thought!
But the former chairman,
Costello, is now president
of the World Bank...*
Plus, their stock price is
high, and their dividends
aren't bad...
What on earth is
Miller thinking?!
The New
York Stock
Exchange

* WORLD BANK: Popular name for the International Bank for Reconstruction and Development, which began operation in 1946 under the Bretton Woods agreement. Founded initially to finance postwar reconstruction, its main function now is to finance industrial development in less developed countries.

CLOSE ENCOUNTERS OF THE THIRD KIND
Sell! Sell!!
They're saddled with irrecoverable energy loans!!
Sell Bank Americana!!
Their clients in Mexico and Brazil are defaulting!!
The farm crisis could push 'em over the edge!!
They've cut dividends for the first time in 53 years!!
Trading's been halted!!
Manhattan Trust's making a takeover bid!!
ROARRR
They're about to announce a formal offer!

Manhattan Trust
will offer $18 per share of Bank Americana stock!
Eighteen dollars?!
We are also filing an application with the Federal Reserve Board to approve the merger!
That's incredibly high!
I hear Manhattan has $2.7 billion ready to spend on the buyout!
So if he gets his way, Miller the disowned son is going to end up taking over daddy's farm, eh?!

U.S. BANK FAILURES: In 1987 American banks were failing at twice the pace of the previous year, due primarily to simultaneous recessions in agriculture, energy, and real estate. Even the biggest banks were staggering under a burden of bad loans.

Bank Americana
Bank Americana
— The Executive Suite
That sonofabitch Miller!!
Why don't we turn the tables on him
and take over Manhattan Trust,
Chairman Costello?!
That sort of thinking is what's gotten you into trouble, Abbott!!
You've done a lousy job of running the show ever since I left for the World Bank!

You put off investing in electronic banking! You made too many bad loans to energy interests and underdeveloped countries...
But the last straw was when you rescheduled* those third world loans!
C-can't you have the World Bank take those loans over for us?!
You know I can't do that!
That's a blatant conflict of interest!
You're fired, Abbott!!
Imbecile!!
...!!
I'll come back and do the job myself!!
Have the Board of Directors issue a statement rejecting the merger.
Then sell off our unprofitable subsidiaries!
Meanwhile, I'll buy some time by getting the FRB to hold up approval of the merger application...

* RESCHEDULING: An extension of the due date for repayment of a loan, often requested by debtor nations unable to pay off their debts.

And issue a press release announcing a reorganization plan and my return as Chairman!
I'll be damned if I'll let this takeover go through!!
>URK<
The Chairman's office, Manhattan Trust
Our takeover bid has gotten nowhere!
With Costello's return as Chairman, the shareholders have stopped selling off their Bank Am stock!
Costello — that bastard!!
Fine, we'll offer $30 per share!!
T-that's ridiculous!!
We'll lose our shirts if we buy it at $30!!

We'd barely break even at $25!
If we pay any more than that,
Our bank will be dragged down with those debtor countries!!
No we won't!
Make another offer at $30 — and tell the Bank Am executives they'll get an average $200 thou a head for their golden parachute!!*
......
Then, we'll manipulate the shareholders into suing Bank Am management —
for breach of trust in rejecting a generous offer for a company on the verge of bankruptcy!!
Tokyo: the Ministry of Finance
NO TAXIS BEYOND THIS POINT

* GOLDEN PARACHUTE: A contract guaranteeing severance pay to top executives when their company is taken over by another company. In the U.S., golden parachutes of $10 million are not unusual.

Office of the Banking Bureau Director
Manhattan Trust has upped its takeover bid for Bank Americana to $30 per share.
They're also prepared to offer some very generous golden parachutes, it appears.
Hmm....
So the second largest bank in America is on the ropes, is it!
The U.S. government can't afford to let 'em go under...
But when you consider the extent of their bad loans to debtor nations in Latin America,
this won't be your standard-issue bailout by a long shot...
So why does a smaller bank like Manhattan Trust want to acquire an expensive albatross like that?!
I've been wondering the same thing.
Chairman Miller seems to have a certain guru-like charisma...
He may well have convinced a bunch of investors to fork out a lot of money for this.
An international speculators' cabal, eh?
HA HA HA!
Yep, something like that would certainly come in handy!

But even if there were such a group, they'd hardly be likely to bet their money on a sure loser!
Exactly!
>SNORT<
That's why propping up Bank Am is such a thankless task!
I see where Costello has returned from the World Bank to take charge of reorganization... I wonder how he's doing.
That could trigger a worldwide depression if he can't pull it off!
Japan is already
recycling its hard-earned dollars by using 'em to buy up U.S. Treasury bonds!
— Thanks to which the U.S. is able to cover its huge budget deficit!*
It's also keeping the dollar from dropping.
But meanwhile, the U.S.
continues to operate in the red,
and the dollar gets weaker and weaker!

* U.S. BUDGET DEFICIT: America revised its high- interest, strong-dollar policy after the G5 meeting in late 1985, but its budget remained deep in the red. Pessimists at the time projected a deficit of $1 trillion by 1990. [The deficit peaked at $290 billion in 1992 and has declined since then — Ed.]

If Japan stopped buying Treasury bonds, people would try to dump their dollars and switch to yen and Deutschmarks...
Then we'd be looking at a serious global crisis.
...So Japan has to keep buying U.S. Treasuries even as they depreciate into worthless scrap!
We're like a wife who has to keep handing money over to her prodigal husband...
because she knows a divorce would ruin both of them!
The Planning Office of Goyo Bank
We can only hope the man of the house will start pulling his own weight
and stop printing bogus money to tide himself over!

With the yen rising so fast now, we can't afford to buy U.S. bonds anymore!
The interest can't keep up with the soaring yen, so it's a losing proposition!
Sounds like we're better off buying real estate for the time being...
Fine, let's stay out of the next round of bidding for Treasuries.
I'll tell the Portfolio Department!
If we move fast, they're bound to appreciate!
Why don't we buy some downtown building sites instead?
Huh! It's getting harder and harder to spend all our money!
I hear Goyo Trust and Goyo Casualty aren't purchasing bonds this time either.
Okay, let's use Goyo Land as a front again...
I'll get right on it!

POLITICAL BUSINESS CYCLES: Today the macroeconomic policies of government play a major role in a nation's economy. Since voters tend to choose politicians who serve their economic interests, the party in power will attempt to create a boom before an election.

The Treasury bond* auction desk at the Federal Reserve Bank of New York

* TREASURY BONDS: Long-term U.S. Treasury securities (also known as Treasuries), with maturities of 5 to 30 years. Other Treasuries include Treasury bills, with maturities of up to 1 year, and Treasury notes, with maturities of 1 to 5 years.

That's odd — the number of bidders has really dropped off.
Especially the Japanese... What the hell's going on?!
Listen, if we open up for bids now, Treasuries will take a nosedive!
Hello, Al?
Hardly any Japanese are participating...
Whaddaya think we should do?!
The Chairman's office, Manhattan Trust
Sounds like we're accumulating stock at a healthy pace!
HEH HEH HEH!
$5 billion should be enough to cover our stock buyup.
Yes...
But they have about $10 billion outstanding in bad loans to Latin America!
How do you intend to deal with that?!
HAW!
If we get paid back later on, they're not really bad loans, now, are they?!
We just have to bide our time.

You Japanese are always so impatient. Bankers have to take the long view!
Well, sure, if the market improves for primary industry products, they'll be able to pay off their debts —
but no one can guarantee that's going to happen!
Well, *we* know it will — according to some top-secret data I happen to have!
Th-that sounds like some sort of fortune-telling mumbo- jumbo!
Economics is a cyclical phenomenon...
You've heard of Kondratieff's 55-year cycle, no doubt?
Of course — the theory that economic booms and busts repeat every 55 years...
But that assumes the occurrence of wars, technological breakthroughs, inventions and the like...
No one can predict the actual timing!
But suppose we *know* the cycle is guaranteed to repeat every 55 years?!
>CHUCKLE<

What?!
You're saying it's okay to defer the repayment of third world loans until the next, supposedly inevitable economic upturn...?!
We'll defer collection of that $10 billion for 30 years. Instead, we'll underwrite 30-year government bonds issued by the debtor countries.
Exactly!
— Making sure, of course, that the interest they pay is high enough to make it worth our while!
Okay, that sounds fine in theory — but it's awfully risky in practice! What happens if those countries aren't back on their feet in 30 years?!
Well, in the meantime, those high-interest Latin American bonds will be a tasty treat in themselves!
I should have no trouble drumming up the $15 billion we need to cover both our takeover costs *and* the banquet fee!!
I'm flying to Switzerland tomorrow to talk to some folks who wish to partake in the feast.

TOTAL THIRD WORLD DEBT: The World Bank had $1.035 trillion in outstanding loans to developing countries in 1986. By 1987 this had risen to $1.08 trillion.

These speculators who follow you with such devotion are a complete mystery to me, Chairman!
Hee hee hee...
SUNSPOT DATA
SUNSPOT DATA
......!?
Switzerland

An expensive resort hotel overlooking the Aare River in Bern...
SUNSPOT DATA
SUNSPOT DATA
SUNSPOT DATA

COUNTRY RISK: The degree of risk a financial institution assumes in lending to a given country. As insurance against bad debt losses due to war, nationalization, etc., banks tend to charge higher interest on loans to risky nations.

SUNSPOT
DATA
The White House, Washington, D.C.
Bank Americana's in deep doo-doo, sir — they're saddled with a massive volume of bad loans to Latin America.
Even so, we can't afford to let the second largest bank in the country go belly-up!

That would precipitate a worldwide panic!
Well, Manhattan Trust's already bought up a good chunk of their stock...
and the Fed intends to give its blessing to the merger!
Costello, the ex-World Bank president, has asked us not to approve the merger.
But this isn't just a problem affecting one bank any longer.
Actually, we'd be better off getting the Japanese to acquire our unsound banks, instead of using American capital.
Every time there's a recession, his bank just grows bigger...
...Miller always seems to be buying up risky banks, doesn't he!
That would recycle some of those Japanese dollars back here, at least...
HMPH!
Japan is so damn self-centered —
it doesn't have any kind of global outlook at all!

EASTERN EUROPEAN DEBT: Brazil's default on interest payments on its debts cast a pall over Poland, Yugoslavia and other European debtor nations, who feared a change in the lending policies of the West.

Yeah, the other day the Japanese suddenly dropped out of the bidding for Treasuries. Scared the hell out of me!
Economically Japan's all grown up, yet it still behaves like a little kid!
Last year the Japanese bought $100 billion's worth of Treasuries.
If they take their money and run off to Europe or somewhere, we'll go bankrupt!
That means they took on half of our budget deficit!
We won't be able to operate in the red anymore...
...So we have no choice but to get Japan to keep buying our bonds, eh.
Well, they practically get a free ride on defense, so why shouldn't they do their share to stabilize the world's economy?!
Then it's agreed — we'll lean on Japan to continue buying Treasuries!
I'll fly to Japan and talk to Prime Minister Nakasone directly.
All in strictest secrecy, of course!

If you slap Japan hard enough, they always flinch!
But you've gotta slap 'em *hard*, now!
WHAP
Tokyo
An *exclusive* restaurant in Akasaka

CONDITIONALITY: When the IMF makes a loan to a debtor nation, it attaches certain conditions — e.g. austerity policies, budget cuts, anti-inflation measures, conversion to a floating exchange rate — and pegs its loans to progress in meeting these requirements.

...Prevent global crisis!
...Bear your share of the burden!
...U.S.-Japanese cooperation!!
......
Residence of the Prime Minister, Nagata-cho

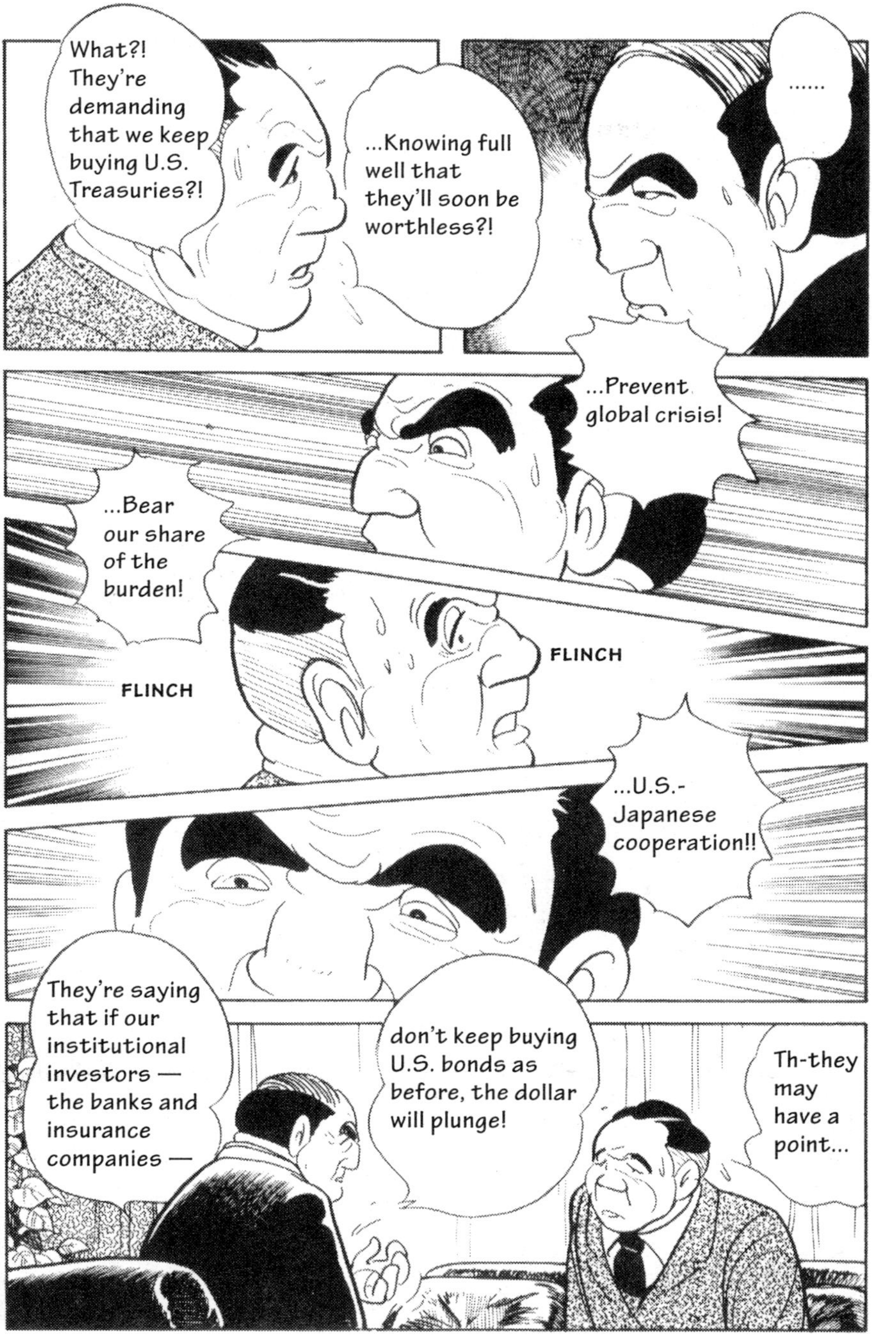
What?! They're demanding that we keep buying U.S. Treasuries?!
...Knowing full well that they'll soon be worthless?!
......
...Prevent global crisis!
...Bear our share of the burden!
FLINCH
FLINCH
...U.S.-Japanese cooperation!!
They're saying that if our institutional investors — the banks and insurance companies —
don't keep buying U.S. bonds as before, the dollar will plunge!
Th-they may have a point...

DEBT SERVICE (DS) RATIO: Debt repayments as a percentage of export earnings. The DS ratio of developing countries crossed the "danger" threshold of 15% in 1984, rising to 16.2%. Half of these payments currently consist of interest.

Well, if the American economy does recover, their Treasury bonds will be a safe, profitable investment, won't they?!
...So they want us to order our banks
to start buying Treasuries again, do they?
Right —
as "our share of the burden of ensuring global economic stability"...
I'm afraid we have no choice.
......
The Christmas holidays are coming up in the U.S., and we have the New Year holiday here... so we'd better get on this right away.
Please get the word out to the big banks!
I'll do my best..
I'm counting on you!

New York: the Century Hyatt Hotel
KNOCK
KNOCK
Hello, Homma-san!
Sawako! Good to see you!
Actually, I was planning to pay *you* a visit...
No, no! Over on this side of the ocean,
I should be looking after you!

JAPANESE BOND TRADING IN NEW YORK: A rise in bond market prices due to the strong yen and lower interest rates has spurred trading in Japanese government bonds in New York. Major U.S. banks and life insurance companies have begun investing in Japanese bonds.

This was a rather sudden trip for you, wasn't it?
Yep, I didn't get much advance warning this time.
I don't have anything here, so why don't we go downstairs for a cup of coffee?
I'll be ready in a minute, so please make yourself comfortable.
Wha-?!
SUNSPOT DATA
Homma-san!
I-is this your book?!
Oh, that? That's a regular publication on sunspot data I get from the Sunspot Observatory in Brussels.
I didn't know you were interested in astronomy!
You know, my boss is always carrying this same pamphlet around!

Well, you see, there's a revolutionary new theory about business cycles that pulls together all the previous cycle theories —
it's quite remarkable!
Business cycle theory? I've heard of the capital investment cycle,
where plant and equipment investment* rises and falls in an 11-year pattern...
Well, that's because the economic life of machinery and equipment is 11 years.
But still,
that doesn't explain why businesses throughout Japan all replace their machinery at the same time,
which is what creates the pattern in the first place!
I see what you mean — that *is* odd...
Here, take a look at this chart.

* PLANT AND EQUIPMENT INVESTMENT: The portion of a company's capital investment put into factories, machinery, equipment etc. Japan's postwar economic growth was fueled by its manufacturers' technical innovations and drive to invest in plant and equipment.

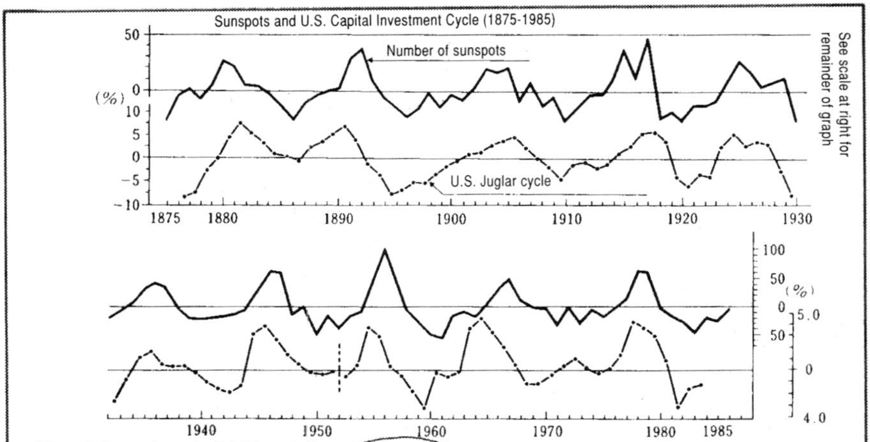
Sunspots and U.S. Capital Investment Cycle (1875-1985)
Number of sunspots
U.S. Juglar cycle
See scale at right for remainder of graph
(%)
50
0
10
5
0
−5
−10
1875
1880
1890
1900
1910
1920
1930
100
50
0
50
(%)
5.0
0
4.0
1940
1950
1960
1970
1980
1985
(This and other graphs are by Yuji Shimanaka.)

Jevons was the first to point out the correlation between business cycles and sunspots.
That's what you see in this graph.
W.S. Jevons, the 19th century British economist?
Right. But after him, the theory was forgotten. Then, in 1977, someone discovered there was a 55-year cycle of fluctuations in sunspot period and amplitude.
If you take five 11-year sunspot cycles,
they form one big wave...
So does that wave
match the Kondratieff wave?!

...Why, they're almost a perfect fit!
......!!
The 55-year sunspot cycle is called the Yoshimura cycle, after the man who discovered it.
Solar activity really does have a 55 year cycle, doesn't it...

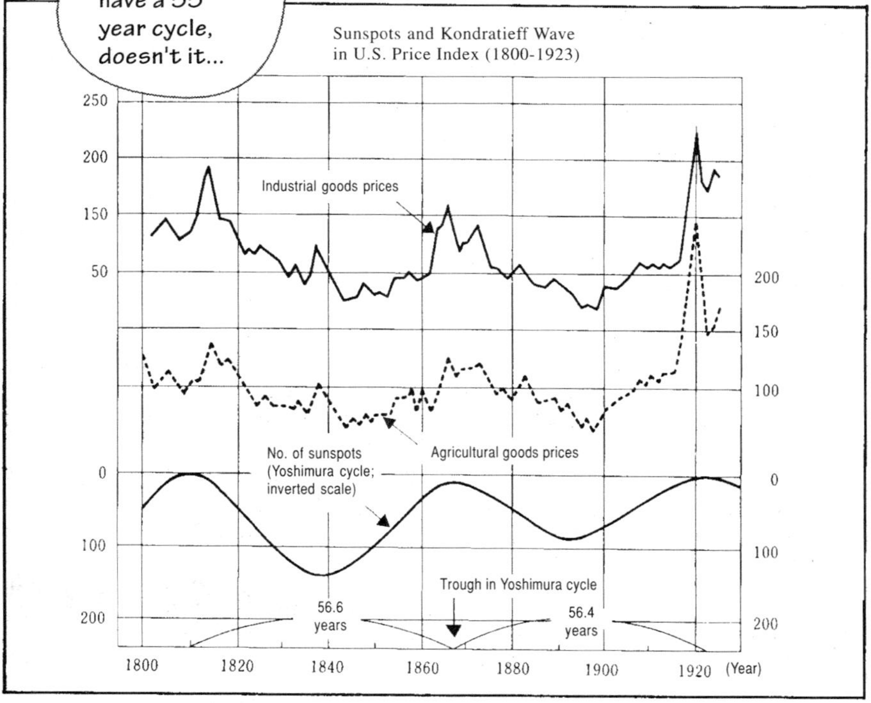
Sunspots and Kondratieff Wave in U.S. Price Index (1800-1923)
Industrial goods prices
Agricultural goods prices
No. of sunspots (Yoshimura cycle; inverted scale)
Trough in Yoshimura cycle
56.6 years
56.4 years
250
200
150
50
0
100
200
1800
1820
1840
1860
1880
1900
1920
(Year)

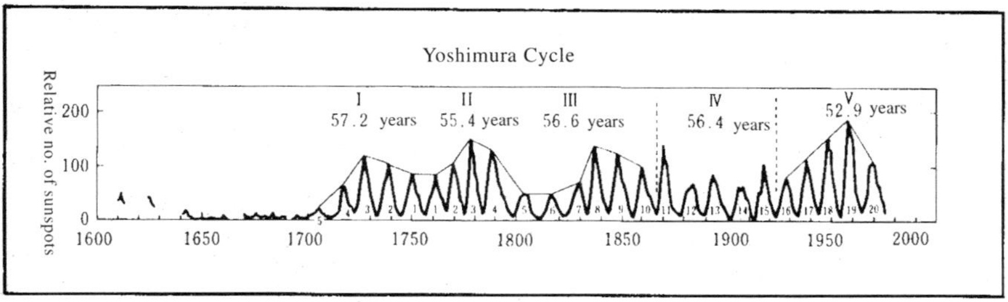
Yoshimura Cycle
Relative no. of sunspots
I 57.2 years
II 55.4 years
III 56.6 years
IV 56.4 years
V 52.9 years
0
100
200
1600
1650
1700
1750
1800
1850
1900
1950
2000

An economist named Shimanaka* determined that the Yoshimura cycle perfectly matches the Kondratieff wave.
So I refer to the economic dimension of the Yoshimura cycle as the "Shimanaka cycle"...
Yoshimura Cycle
I 57.2 years
II 55.4 years
III 56.6 years
1750
1850
History had already provided ample proof of Kondratieff's 55-year cycle theory, hadn't it?
But no one understood its cause, so they couldn't use it to predict future trends...
Until now!
It's been proven that for the last 700 million years or so, solar activity has followed regular cycles of 11 and 55 years.**
So that means
we can rely on the accuracy of the Shimanaka cycle in the future as well...?!
That's amazing!
Yep. Sure makes it easy to make money!
Just buy stock in the equipment makers who get their business from capital investment...

* See Yuji Shimanaka, *Taiyo Katsudo to Keiki [Solar Activity and Business Cycles]*, Nihon Keizai Shimbunsha, 1987.

** See G.E. Williams, " Solar Activity Cycles in the Precambrian Era," *Science*, October 1986.

All you have to do is buy at the bottom of the 11-year cycle, and sell at the top!
And companies on the verge of collapse benefit
because they can borrow funds to tide them over, knowing exactly how long it'll be till the next upswing in the cycle!
There are people who've known about this for some time, aren't there!
Homma-san!
If we know for certain that the cycle is always 55 years...
Besides the 55-year cycle in solar activity
Of course!
Like Nostra-damus,* for example?
people have been talking about a 110-year cycle from way back...

* NOSTRADAMUS: French astrologer (1503-66) who served as court physician to King Charles XI. His prophecies, written in verse, have been subject to a variety of interpretations.

It's no wonder he was able to extract some definitive data about cycles out of all that.
The Chinese were aware of cycles, too, if you look at their astrology, or the I Ching...
...But it wasn't till the Yoshimura cycle was discovered ten years ago that all this was scientifically validated...?
Oh yes! He had a huge store of knowledge at his fingertips, both astronomical and historical.
Precisely — which explains the rumors of a sudden proliferation over the last decade of speculator cabals that rely on sunspot data they obtain from Brussels!
I walked off with your book without thinking!
Oh dear!
SUNSPOT DATA
Why don't you keep it? I've already read it!
No problem!
HA
HA
HA!

Hmm... so there really are groups of clever speculators out there —
but you're saying all they do is follow the business cycles caused by sunspot fluctuations?
Well, the sun is the source of our energy here on earth, after all!
It affects the weather, which determines whether harvests are good or bad, which affects economic activity — *even* human activity!
Human activity ?!
Well, for example —
even a physiological phenomenon
like the 27-day menstrual cycle correlates with the rotation of the sun!
The sun's magnetic field affects the magnetism of the earth — which in turn exercises a big influence on human beings!
Here, take a look at this.
......

Economic activity depends on human "vitality," and our vitality fluctuates with the sun's energy, as you can see here!
Infectious Diseases and Geomagnetic Activity (ΣKp) (Jagodzinski et al., 1971)
ΣKp
Geomagnetism
Population (x 1000)
800 600 400
22 18 14
Dys-entery
1950 54 58 62 Year
(This and other graphs are from Maeda, Do Organisms Feel Magnetism?, Kodansha.)
So the sun controls everything, does it?!
Economists, businessmen, even doctors — nowadays everyone should be consulting data on natural phenomena!
ΣKp
Geomagnetism
%
Population (x 1000)
180 140 100 60
24 20 16 12
Scarlet fever
1947 51 55 Year
Chairman Miller has staked his whole strategy for acquiring Bank Americana on the 55-year cycle!
Well, if he's right, the primary industry market should hit bottom and start improving around the year 2000.
If it does, those Latin American countries will prosper again and pay back their debts...
So that's why the Chairman is eagerly buying up loans that appear to be bad —
ΣKp
Geomagnetism
Population (x 1000)
18 14 10
20 16
Smallpox
1938 42 46 50 Year

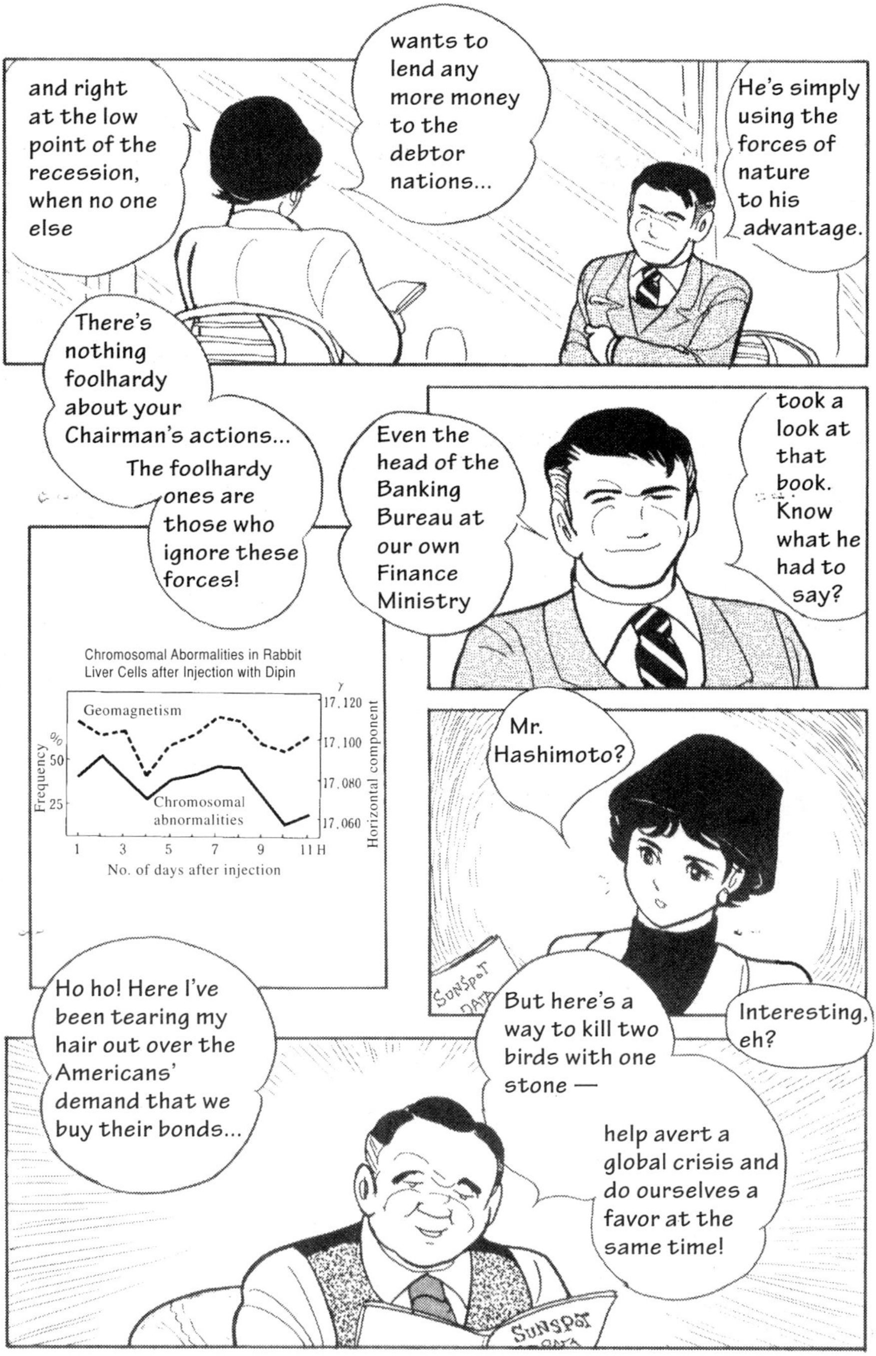
and right at the low point of the recession, when no one else
wants to lend any more money to the debtor nations...
He's simply using the forces of nature to his advantage.
There's nothing foolhardy about your Chairman's actions...
The foolhardy ones are those who ignore these forces!
Even the head of the Banking Bureau at our own Finance Ministry
took a look at that book. Know what he had to say?
Chromosomal Abormalities in Rabbit Liver Cells after Injection with Dipin
Geomagnetism
Chromosomal abnormalities
Frequency %
Horizontal component
No. of days after injection
Mr. Hashimoto?
SUNSPOT DATA
Ho ho! Here I've been tearing my hair out over the Americans' demand that we buy their bonds...
But here's a way to kill two birds with one stone —
Interesting, eh?
help avert a global crisis and do ourselves a favor at the same time!
SUNSPOT DATA

GETTING DEBTOR NATIONS BACK IN THE BLACK: To spur use of the yen to assist less developed countries, Japan's Finance Ministry announced that as of FY1987 it would purchase bonds from foreign governments and the World Bank with funds from the private sector and the government's special account.

What did he mean, exactly?
Japan should lend its money to the debtor countries
in place of the Yanks!
Oh, I see!
You mean Japan should take over the bad loans U.S. banks have made to the third world, right?!
RIGHT!
Instead of using our dollars to buy U.S. bonds,
we can buy government bonds from Mexico, Brazil, and the like — that's a more effective way to shore up the global economy!
Look, it's snowing! I wonder if New York is in for a white Christmas...

That reminds me, Sawako —
Do you think you'll be home in time for Professor Funaoka's New Year tea ceremony?
Yes, I certainly hope so!
Good! I'll see you there, then!
That gives me something to look forward to.
......
The White House
What?! You say the Japanese are aggressively lending to the worst debtor countries?!

LATIN AMERICAN DEBT: In 1985, Brazil ranked worst among Latin American debtor nations with $107.3 billion in outstanding debts, followed by Mexico with $99 billion, Argentina with $50.8 billion, Venezuela with $33.6 billion, and Chile with $21 billion.

They say they're doing it "to ensure global economic stability"...
Well, that's one helluva switcheroo for them! Whaddaya s'pose made 'em suddenly see the light?!
I don't like the sound of it...
That's not all.
A Japanese bank, Goyo, says it wants to buy Bank Americana!
They've already submitted a formal application, I'm told!
And they'd leave Costello in charge at the top, too...
WHAT!?
If they're true to their word,
HMM...
That would certainly keep Costello happy.
Hey, sounds like a plan!!
But what do we do about Manhattan Trust's offer?!

Manhattan? Put 'em off by telling 'em there's a potential antitrust problem we've gotta look into!
Meanwhile, we let the Japanese buy out Bank Am!!
The Chairman's office, Manhattan Trust
G-Goyo Bank is offering $35 per share for Bank Americana?!
What?!
And the government is saying our own offer may violate antitrust law?!
That's right.
We've already received a notice from the SEC...*
Arrghh!!
TREMBLE
Th-there's something going on here —
something damn fishy, if you ask me!!

* SEC: The Securities and Exchange Commission, the U.S. regulatory agency that oversees the securities business. The Securities Bureau of the Finance Ministry serves the same function in Japan, but the SEC has greater powers of enforcement.

Chairman Miller!
You shouldn't let yourself get so excited — it's bad for your health!
MOAN...
SHADDUP!!
Fine, I'll be going now...
SUNSPOT DATA
H-hold on a sec, Sawako!
URK!
W-what's that book you've got there...?!
Oh, this?
This is the Japanese Bible, Chairman!

WHA-?!
SUNSPOT DATA
Since ancient times,
the Japanese have worshipped the sun goddess, Amaterasu...
This booklet contains an update of that ancient wisdom, you might say...
Correct me if I'm wrong, but you appear to worship the same deity yourself, Chairman —
don't you?!
Y-you could say that...

BRAZIL'S SUSPENSION OF INTEREST PAYMENTS: Citing insufficient foreign currency reserves, Brazil announced it was suspending interest payments on its external debt in February 1987. The move was indicative of the severity of the third world debt crisis.

Well, I'll be on my way.
......
AARGHH!!
Now the Japanese are following sunspot cycles too! I'm screwed!!
Kennedy Airport
Thanks for coming to see me off, Sawako.
Well, I felt bad we weren't able to get together again while you were here...

I'm glad we'll be meeting again soon, and in more relaxed circumstances!
Me, too...
Oh yeah — Sawako!
I've got a sequel to that funny story I told you a while back!
Care to hear it?
...A sequel?!
Ottawa, Canada
1988: the 14th Summit Conference

We Japanese are well aware of our responsibilities toward the global economy, and we pledge to do our utmost to ensure economic stability worldwide...
In particular, we are prepared to move aggressively to deal with the problem of outstanding third world debt!
CLAP
CLAP
Noboru-san!
As Yasu's successor, I expect you're a tough mah-jongg player too!
Oh no, hardly!

I'm a believer in international cooperation, not winner-take-all!
And I've brought along this handy little device for the purpose!!
But in exchange, I propose we use yen to settle our bets!
I have Margaret's and Francois' support in this regard...

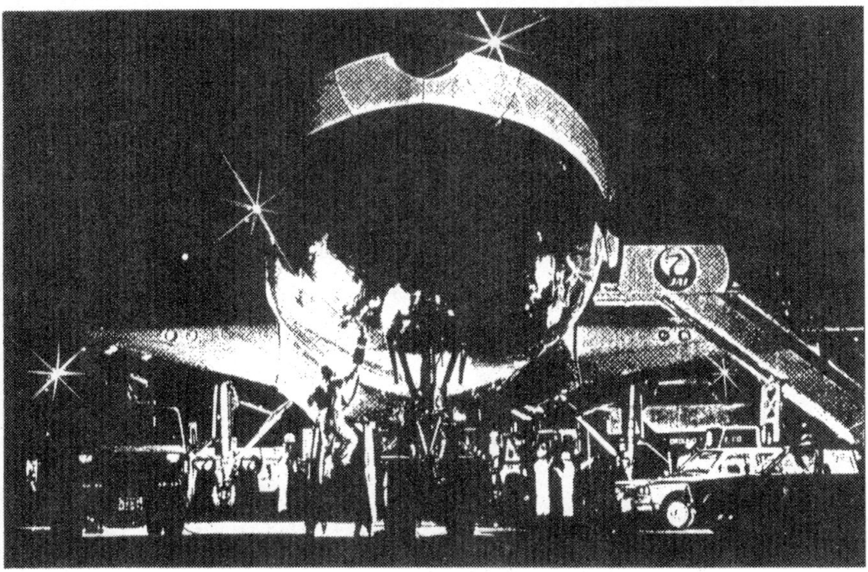

BAKER PLAN: A plan for bailing out debtor nations proposed by U.S. Treasury Secretary James Baker at a joint IMF-World Bank meeting in fall 1985. It was agreed that private banks in Japan, the U.S. and Europe would lend Mexico up to $7.7 billion.

HOTEL PLATON

2-1, KIOI-CHO, CHIYODA-KU
TOKYO, JAPAN
PHONE : 03-379-5459

When the industrial revolution swept England in the 1760s, it was accompanied by the onset of a mysterious cycle of business booms and slumps. In their attempts to solve the riddle of the business cycle, economists have advanced a number of theories. Economists today recognize the following four types of cycle:

(1) Juglar Cycle: An 11-year cycle, also known as the capital investment cycle because it is attrib uted to the average economic life of machinery and equipment, which is about 11 years.

(2) Kitchin Cycle: A cycle of a bit less than four years, also known as the inventory cycle because it is attributed to fluctuations in inventory investment.

(3) Kondratieff Wave: A long, 55-year cycle discovered by the Russian economist Kondratieff, attributed to four factors: technical innovation, gold production, war, and agriculture.

(4) Kuznets Cycle: A cycle of approximately 22 years, also known as the building cycle because it is attributed to a 22-year cycle in residential and commercial building construction.

The existence of the Juglar cycle has been confirmed by trends in both the U.S. and Japan over several decades, both before and after the war, but I still don't understand what causes it. Why does the confidence of businessmen wax and wane every 11 years? It seems impossible to explain except as an effect of the 11- year cycle of the source of our energy, the sun. After all, it's a fact that the sun has exerted control over all living creatures since creation. In that respect, depriving ourselves of protection from the sun by sending CFCs into the atmosphere may prove an even greater folly on humanity's part than the invention of nuclear weapons... It seems that we have no choice but to view humanity and nature in a cosmic context! Now, that's a rather romantic, exciting notion, don't you think?

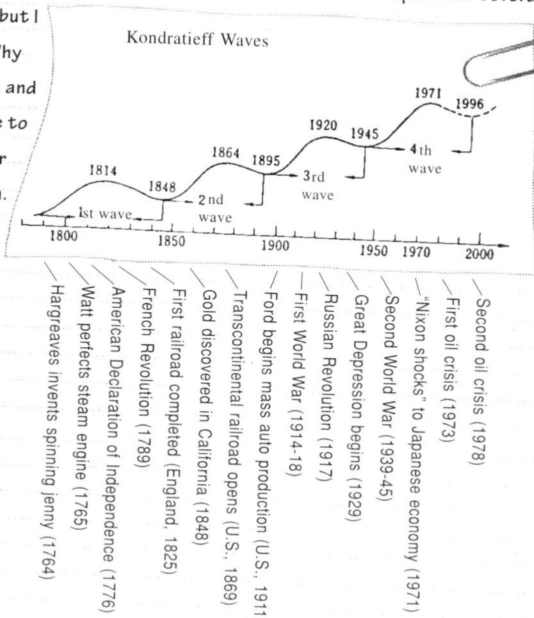

⑤ *Epilogue*

The Sun intones, in ancient tourney
With brother-spheres, a rival song,
Fulfilling its predestined journey,
With march of thunder moves along.
Its aspect gives the angels power,
Though none can ever solve its ways;
The lofty works beyond us tower,
Sublime as on the first of days.

— Goethe, *Faust*

Kyoto:
the
Funaoka
residence

SUN WORSHIP: Worship of the heavenly body that most directly affects human lives has been a common practice at least since the days of the Incas and the ancient Egyptians. The Japanese myth of the sun goddess Amaterasu Omikami is one such example.

Actually, I came to say goodbye, Professor.
What's the matter, Suzuki? You look pretty glum for New Year's Day!
Well, y'see, I, uh—
I've been transferred to our U.S. plant.
...I see.
But doesn't that suit you a lot more than the sales work you've been doing?

Well, yes, I suppose so...
What about your family? Are they going too?
Your mother's living with you, as I recall...
I'll have to leave her with my brother. I can only take the wife and kids with me.
It's been real hard on my mother...
So Matsudai's building a plant in the States...
What about their plant here, then?
Oh, they'll be closing it down.
Scrap Japan,
build in the U.S.A — that's how it goes.
Guess there's really no way to stop the hollowing out* of our industries, then...
I'm not sure moving to the States will do a bottom-ranked company like ours any good.
But our president says

* HOLLOWING OUT: Pundits warn of the "hollowing out" of Japanese industry as companies increasingly move production overseas, leading to factory closures and fewer jobs at home.

"Better to die in America than sit waiting for the end in Japan"!
But if you lose that gamble,
Matsudai employees and their families will suffer...
Well, we don't have much choice.
It's as if we're being swept along by a great wave.
It's out of my hands, so I'll just do the best I can.
"America or bust," as they say!
......
And to that end, we've got to discard our irrational Japanese sentimentality!
As bankers, I believe our top priority should always be to maximize profits!

Japan got stabbed in the back by the Euro-American banking clique over the Latin American debt problem...
But we've got to keep on pushing against the old boys' club — even if we have to do it single-handedly!
......
Sawako!
Oh,it's you, Hiroshi!
First time I've ever seen you in a kimono — you look absolutely stunning!

TECHNOLOGY EXPORT: The export of domestically developed technology in exchange for equivalent value. Examples include blueprints, proprietary information on plant construction, and various types of engineering and consulting knowhow.

You know, you completely threw me for a loop over that whole Taigen Bank brouhaha!
Oh, come on, I did no such thing!
Besides, you've more than made up for it with this Bank Americana caper! Shall we call it a draw?
......
Uh, by the way,
Sawako...
Yes?
Um, actually,
I'll be staying here in Kyoto tonight, and I was wondering
if you had any plans for the evening...?
I promised some friends I'd see them tonight...
Oh dear! I'm sorry —

Oh. That's too bad.
I was hoping we could find time for a good leisurely chat for a change...
>GIGGLE<
Well, I'm sure there'll be other opportunities!
......
...I'm sick and tired of being pushed around by politicians!
Always scavenging for pork for their districts —
>HIC<
and leaving us holding the bag!
Now I understand why you lost your faith in the political process, Professor —
quitting all your public positions,
— just like that!! Even the Economic Deliberation Council!
Ha ha ha!
It wasn't really like that!
I started to lose faith in myself as an economist
around the time of the oil crises, when excess liquidity* became a problem!
Well, but
all your warnings to the policymakers fell on deaf ears!

* EXCESS LIQUIDITY: When the money supply exceeds demand in a financial market. A strong flow of foreign currency into a country increases domestic liquidity, but this can trigger inflation, requiring monetary adjustments by the central bank.

The pols only care about one thing, getting votes.
So what did we wind up with? Rampant inflation!
>SNORT<
True enough.
Just goes to show — there's a helluva gap between economics in the ivory tower and policy in the political arena!
Yes?
I'm curious, Sawako...
How do you feel about
Mr. Okada?
F-feel about him...?!
And yet —
It's obvious that he really likes you.

he seems to have something holding him back
that makes it hard for him to tell you.
......
It's not just sunspots, you know.
But he's young, single, a rising star in a top firm... quite a catch, don't you think?
The aurora exhibits an 11-year cycle, too.
Nowadays economics sounds more and more like a branch of heliology!
Yeah, if that theory about the 11-year cycle doesn't hold up, the banking industry's gonna be in big trouble!
Well, I don't know about you,
but the realization that human activities are governed by these huge natural cycles
sometimes makes me feel like all our rushing around is much ado about nothing!
......

I don't know if I'll be here to appreciate your wonderful tea ceremony skills this time next year, Sawako.
What?!
Yep, that's right — Homma is going to be quitting the Finance Ministry!
Quitting?!
You've gotta be kidding!
What the hell for?!
Actually, I'm the culprit who put him up to it.
He's going to set up a research institute
to work on a new economic theory, something called Total Human Science...

"Total Human Science" ...?!
Well, I've been thinking about this for a while. The more I studied international conflicts in all their permutations,
the more it seemed to me that conventional academic disciplines just weren't going to come up with the answers... Then I ran across the sunspot theory — that really blew everything out of the water for me.
No. of sunspots (Yoshimura cycle)
So I finally decided to put my money where my mouth is!
To make a long story short,
I think we need to develop a comprehensive science of humanity — an eco-economics
with a broad perspective that encompasses heliology, geomagnetics, medicine, psychology, sociology...
Fine, but what about money?
Research institutes don't come cheap, y'know!
Oh, that's working out just fine!
Homma and I have been talking to a number of friends of ours, corporate sponsors...

RESEARCH EXPENDITURES: In 1985 the U.S. spent 25.95 trillion yen on research and development, both government and private. Japan spent only a third that amount: 8.89 trillion yen, about what the U.S. government spent on defense research alone.

F-friends?!
Then why didn't you talk to us?!
No need to stand on ceremony!
My bank would gladly help finance a project like yours!
Banks are part of the information industry now, too, y'know...
Right, Mr. Hashimoto?!
Hm? Uh, right, I guess so...
HA
HA
HA
...
Of course, we were planning to contact you as soon as our plans were a little more definite!
But we didn't want any strings attached.
That's another reason Homma's quitting the Ministry — we don't want a conflict of interest here...
Meanwhile, I'm going to be taking off soon on a tour of research institutions around the world — do a little headhunting...*
Yep, if Homma's research achieves what we hope it will,

* HEADHUNTING: Recruiting talented personnel from a rival company or a different field. Some 10,000 professional headhunters were doing business in the late eighties in the U.S., where the practice began.

the day may come when sunspot and geomagnetic data are part of the weather forecast on TVs and radios everywhere!
That information could be put to use by hospitals, stock markets, securities companies — you name it!

...And who knows, maybe getting a better view of the big picture will help us solve some of the problems we face today!

You gave me a real shock, Homma-san!
It's not just your new research project,
but this drive of yours to create new challenges for yourself...
Heh heh! You mean, you didn't think an old geezer like me had it in him...!
No, it's not that at all!
It's just such a contrast with my own life!

I feel like I'm doing my job from force of habit — I've lost sight of any goals I had...
Cheer up, Sawako!
You've just been working too hard!
Try to relax a little, and take a look at the world around you!
H-Homma-san...
I-I'm going to miss you so much...
Y-you are?!

SUPERWOMAN SYNDROME: A term coined by the American psychologist Marjorie Shaevitz to describe the tendency of career women to exhaust themselves in the pursuit of perfection in both their professional and personal lives.

......!!
Would you mind terribly...
if I stayed with you tonight...?
HO HO HO
HA HA HA

I'd like that very much, Sawako...

MAGNETIC STORM: Marked, irregular disturbances in the magnetism of the earth. These often occur in 27-day cycles, as well as around the vernal and autumnal equinoxes, and are thought to be related to fluctuations in sunspots and the solar corona.

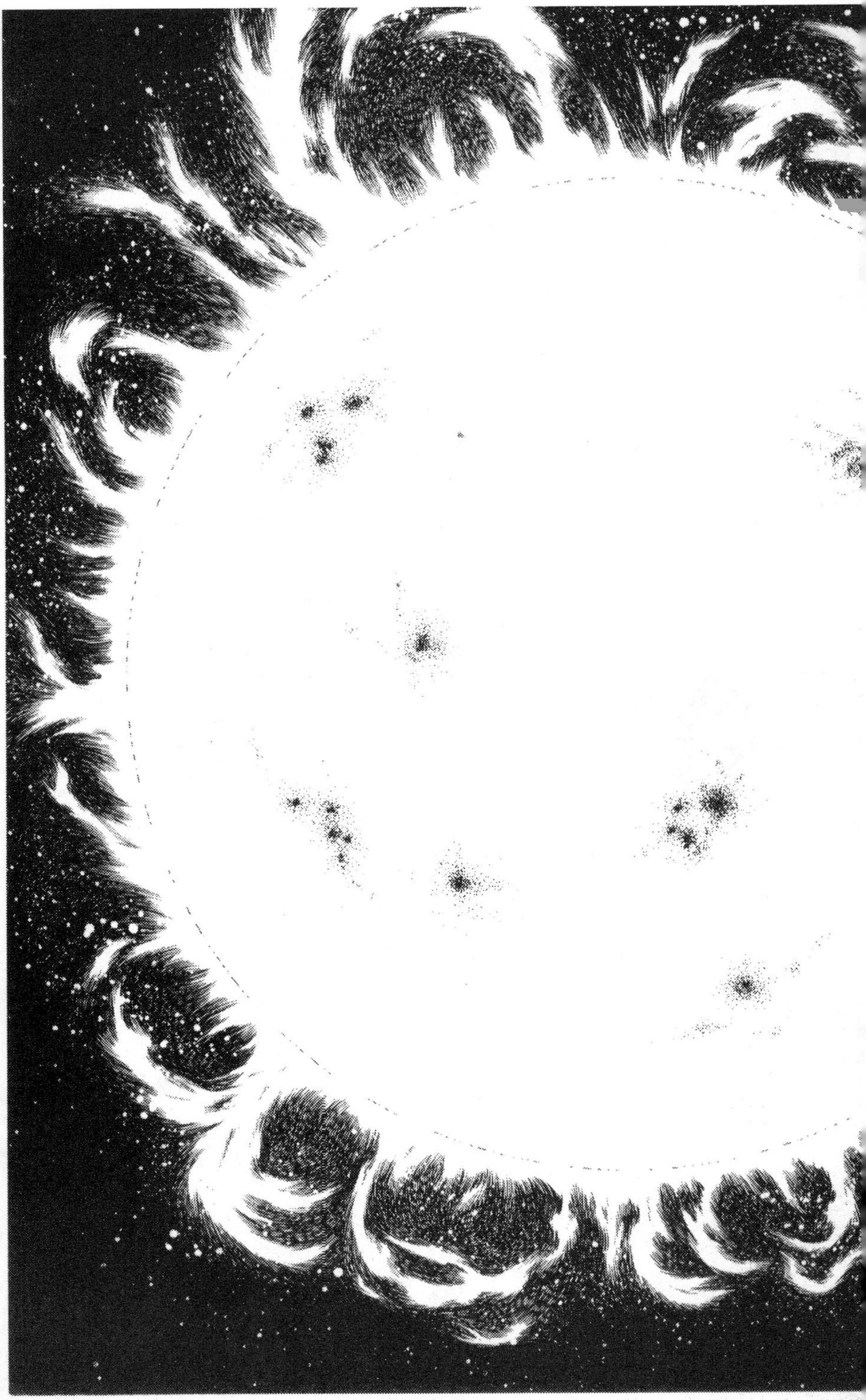

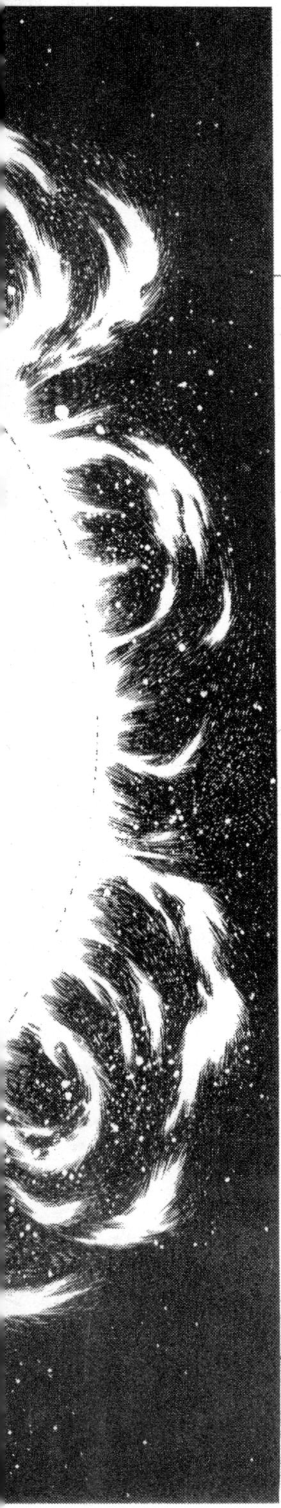

HOTEL PLATON

2-1, KIOI-CHO, CHIYODA-KU
TOKYO, JAPAN
PHONE : 03-379-5459

"Spring is short! Who says
our life's immortal?"
I said, and made his hands
caress my strong breasts
Akiko *

* Akiko Yosano, poet (1878-1942)
(English translation by Hiroaki Sato)